Gifts from the Bridegroom

Inheriting a Beauty that Lasts

Karen,
He cherishes
you with an
amazing love.
Jan Brunette
2006

By Jan Brunette

Gifts from the Bridegroom
ISBN 1-930285-08-6

Published by The Master Design
PO Box 17865
Memphis, TN 38187-0865
Info@masterdesign.org
www.masterdesign.org

Printed by Bethany Press International in the USA.

JJ

To my earthly bridegroom, Duane
Thanks for your many years of commitment
and service to the Lord

CONTENTS

Diligence 1

Compassion 9

A Strong Work Ethic 15

Wisdom 21

Radiance 27

Purity 33

Reverence 40

Gentleness 47

A Quiet Spirit 53

Freedom from Fear 59

A Trusting Heart 66

Unrelenting Love 72

His Fullness 78

Eternal Life 84

Chapter Bible Studies 91

INTRODUCTION

So often in my life I perceive myself as having failed in my role of wife and mother. No matter how much I may have believed that the steps I took and the choices I made were the best possible, in retrospect, I understand that immaturity and lack of knowledge intervened. By holding fast to the faith I possess and the assurance that in all things, God will produce positive effects, I rest in the thought: "I did the best I could with the wisdom I had at the time."

As Christ opened visions and truths of my divine inheritance in His kingdom, I understand more intensely the profuse and abounding love emanating from His loving hand into my life. While mistakes were made, His ever-increasing power and love overpowered and embraced my humanness. Examining Scripture vigorously today, I grasp through His eyes of love the amazing gifts bestowed upon me as His bride. None poured into my life as a result of my own efforts or wisdom or knowledge. Rather, He supplied the goodness, grace, love and power to possess these qualities – first reflected in Himself, then granted to me through His divine Holy Spirit.

Overshadowed by human hurts, pains, and frustrations, I often failed to see the loving discipline and kindness bestowed upon me through the lives of others, especially my husband and children. Perceiving them as the source of conflict and trouble, I refused to point at the potential of His Spirit within me. What was He trying to teach me? How could this situation create in me the Christ-like bride He desired? Did I even notice the changes within as His Spirit molded, shaped and pounded me into a precious jewel in His crown? Only as my faith grew and my yearnings for the presence of Christ in my life accelerated, did I realize it to be one of the greatest rewards of His kingdom.

The gifts the Bridegroom bestows on His bride can seldom be measured by weights and scales. Yet the value is priceless – the result, eternal. Radiating through Christ into the lives of others, these qualities and spiritual rewards explode with a flurry of generous abundance to the lives of others. While some become outwardly valuable in material gains, many are perceived as proceeding from within by the flow of love, generosity, and tenderness showered on others.

Join me in the adventure of your life as you discover the true treasures flowing from the hands of Jesus Christ through the power of His Holy Spirit. He has chosen and called you as His bride. Rejoice as you view His love and power in action through each gift generously spilling into your inward being. You will never regret the journey.

Jan Brunette
Florida, 2002

Chapter 1

DILIGENCE

She possessed dogged determination. None could sway her from the goal. The task, though insurmountable and complicated, only served to enhance her desire to work harder and complete the task. Unfailing love for her family smoothed the difficulties and enabled joy to flood from her being.

Women of today, I call you to that type of ministry to your family. Revealing His strength and possessing His power, set your sights on accomplishing His will. Be like the Proverbs 31 woman, who feared the Lord and remained diligent in all her tasks–thereby accomplishing incredible feats. For example: She works with eager hands, though rough and sore. She brings food from afar (like the corner grocery store or the nearest farmers' market). A feast is set before her family, however swiftly prepared or purchased. With muscles the size of Hercules', she works vigorously. Laboring diligently all day and into the night, she manages to sell her wares and help assist the family income. She is anything but lazy. And joy flows! (Proverbs 31:13-19)

Amazing isn't she? But I hear many of you saying, "I am swamped and overloaded. Hours in the day remain the same, but the labors of my life keep me so busy that fatigue and irritability are a constant part of it. Where is the joy? Where is the strength? Where is the power?"

The workplace demands constant attention and energies. The household chores, the demands of the children, and possibly the expectations of husbands load our already full plate. We wonder how long that "dogged determination" can hold up. Yet we continue day after day.

Although thankful for all the blessings the Lord awards us in our lives, the demands on body and mind overwhelm. "How long, Lord?"

we cry out. "How long must I persist and persevere without help? Give me strength!"

Unable to see beyond the curtains of this life, we hide behind them hoping some magic potion or knight-in-shining-armor will surface and whisk us away from the never- ending labors and demands. In the meantime, most of us remain diligent. We set our hearts on the purpose for which we carry out the demands – that of aiding and supporting the family – and trudge onward one day at a time.

How He grieves! How He desires to carry the load! Yet our stubborn hearts and complaints block the road He must travel. He craves to spend time with us, His bride, but we are too busy to spend time with Him. We fill our days with ball games, shopping, exercise, church activities, and work – whether in the home or out of it. "Never enough time for You, Jesus," we cry. "Can't You see that my only free time is at 4:00 a.m. or 10:00 p.m? Then I am so tired that my mind wanders, my body aches and my heart just isn't in it. There just isn't enough time."

Again He grieves. He reaches out to us and sheds tears of love in our absence. He does not leave. He will not dessert us. Day after day, the Bridegroom waits and waits and waits. "If only your diligence found its rest in Me. If only you chose to seek Me first. I yearn to provide what you lack. I desire to reveal a diligence that brings lasting joy and eternal pleasures. Trust Me. Please, trust Me."

Why do we find it so difficult to turn our eyes heavenward, focus on Him and His Word, and relish the joys found only in Him? Time spent with Him in the here and now brings moments, hours and days of joy and peace. Yet we turn our backs to all that He has to offer. He is proud of our diligence and, in fact, provides strength in abundance, but hangs His head in sorrow when viewing the displacing of it in our lives and in the lives of our loved ones. In the center of His heart is the gentle endurance, the quiet splendor of diligent effort expended for Him. With our best interest at heart, He calls us into His presence and offers all the emotional and spiritual strength we need to serve our family through Him – one day at a time.

Don't hesitate to drop everything and run to Him. This Bridegroom opened the windows of heaven for you. He gave not only energy on your behalf but demonstrated dogged determination as He marched onward toward the cross. Always certain of the result – your salvation and your eternal treasure in heaven – He resolutely and solidly moved forward.

While the days brought heartache and unending demands – He moved onward. In the midst of angry church leaders and misdirected disciples – He continued to keep His face toward Jerusalem. As the exhaustion overtook and fearful followers doubted, He looked ever forward to the cross. It would be His crowning achievement – literally. It would forever take its place in history. His diligent attitude, His steady determination refused to be abated. He had loved ones to rescue. His love, like no other, moved Him.

Therefore *let us fix our eyes on Jesus, the author and perfector of our faith, who for the joy set before him endured the cross, scorning its shame, and sat down at the right hand of the throne of God. Consider him who endured such opposition from sinful men, so that you will not grow weary and lose heart* (Hebrews 12:2-3).

Make Time For Him

Falling down on my knees I ached inside to see the Christ who gave His all for me. Understanding Him to be my Bridegroom – my flawless, loving, accepting Bridegroom – I pleaded for an undivided heart. Often encompassing many desires and emotions, my life seemed shrouded with confusion. My heartfelt needs were spread in so many different directions, none bringing the joy I anticipated.

Trying to please everyone – spreading myself so thin- I was doing a lot and accomplishing little. Or so it seemed. After cleaning the house, I discovered it needed cleaning again. Buying groceries, paying bills, running errands filled my only free day. Fatigue in the evening after a full day's work only brought more fatigue to me again the next day. I began to easily relate to Solomon in Ecclesiastes: *"Meaningless! Meaningless!" says the Teacher. "Utterly meaning-*

less! Everything is meaningless." What does man gain from all his labor at which he toils under the sun...I have seen all the things that are done under the sun, all of them meaningless, a chasing after the wind (vs. 2-3,14).

Guard my life, for I am devoted to you. You are my God; save your servant who trusts in you. Have mercy on me, O Lord, for I call to you all day long. Bring joy to your servant, for to you, O Lord, I lift up my soul. You are forgiving and good, O Lord, abounding in love to all who call on you...Teach me your way, O Lord, and I will walk in your truth; give me an undivided heart that I may fear your name (Psalm 86:2-5,11).

Upon discovering these verses mentioned in Psalm 86, a melodious chord struck my inner being. Reading and rereading it many times, I began to grasp the one diligent effort in life I overlooked. While my job, the housework, the children, and church work absorbed a great deal of my time, it all depended on my own efforts. Pushing myself feverishly, I discovered my own limits were about to be reached. "It's just a matter of time before you crash, Jan," I thought. "It will catch up with you sooner or later."

The words, *I am devoted to you,* filled me with a sense of conviction. How could I repeat those words and yet so seldom seek Him in my daily life? As I trudged, moved, and skipped through my daily routines, I failed to seek Him first. Time spent in His loving temple did not surface. I know He desired my presence and, more than that, He planned to assist me and strengthen me for the loads I carried. But my flesh believed I could go it alone.

For I call to you all day long – that phrase stung like a bee. While I prayed during the difficult times, I seldom called to Him all day long. He certainly did not hold a place of precedence in my mental and spiritual life. My spirit needed food – His food. I failed to use praise and thanksgiving and to lift up holy hands to Him in prayer. That had to change. It would change.

My comfort rested in the knowledge that I was forgiven and good in the sight of the Lord – not because I deserved it but because He is God – a God who *abounds* in love. I had made mistakes. I let my busyness dominate. But in my calling to Him, He forgave, cleansed, renewed, and refreshed. His Spirit would change me. A new Christ-like diligence would surface.

Surrendering my inadequate, haphazard busy schedule into His hands, I prayed, *Teach me your way, O Lord, and I will walk in your truth; give me an undivided heart, that I may fear your name* (Psalm 86:11). Desiring to place Him first in my life, I diligently resolved to set aside a time each day for praise, thanksgiving and worship. That accompanied the requests for the children, for our needs and for my spiritual commitment. Knowing He deserved my praise and respect, I trusted Him for that undivided heart – the heart that diligently seeks Him.

Solomon summed it up beautifully at the end of His book in Ecclesiastes: *Now all has been heard; here is the conclusion of the matter: Fear God and keep his commandments, for this is the whole duty of man* (Ecclesiastes 12:13). Amen and Amen.

Spread It Around

Whatever your hand finds to do, do it with all your might (Ecclesiastes 9:10a). *Let us not become weary in doing good, for at the proper time we will reap a harvest if we do not give up* (Galatians 6:9). *God is not unjust; he will not forget your work and the love you have shown him as you have helped his people and continue to help them. We want each of you to show this same diligence to the very end, in order to make your hope sure. We do not want you to become lazy, but to imitate those who through faith and patience inherit what has been promised* (Hebrews 6:10-12).

I once read a quote by Edward Everett Hale: "I am only one, but I am one. I cannot do everything, but I can do something; and what I can do, that I ought to do – by the grace of God I shall do."[1] Another quote is from Doris Lessing: "It is my belief that talent is plentiful, and that what is lacking is staying power."[2]

These two quotes and the noted Bible verses illustrate the second step in diligence. After first seeking the Lord with all your heart, all your mind and all your soul, the outpouring of that diligent love and energy flows through to others. Centered on His love, His grace, and His staying power, we pray one day at a time to fulfill the ministry and accomplish the goals centered in Him, planned by Him and provided for by Him. Rather than racing here and there, frustrated, lonely, and feeling forsaken, we rest in the assurance that the events of the day are filled with His abundant grace and power. Even the unexpected can be handled with calmness, for our spirit has already been refreshed and prepared for it.

A diligent heart then embraces the generating power of the Holy Spirit. Even though the schedule may be grueling, His Spirit motivates us. A renewed vision for the monotonous may even excite us, as we perceive the blessings of those who are recipients of the Lord's love through us.

I remember a story told to me: An elderly gentleman accepted the often- unacceptable job of washing windows. Week after week, he washed the windows at a particular post office, smiling and singing during the entire process. Finally, an employee of the post office could not help but ask, "How can you be so happy doing such a mundane, boring job?" With a broad smile and a twinkle in his eye, he replied, "The light reflecting from the windows reminds me of the light of Christ that shines in my heart and I cannot but find joy in serving Him and others in this way." What a precious attitude regarding diligence and especially for the joy discovered when in service for Him!

So God desires that His life-flow pass on to others. In the midst of the mundane, the ordinary, or the boring, His joy can explode within us, radiating to others. His glory is revealed. His love is shared.

Stick To It

"If God has called you to a task, determine to complete it, even if you face opposition or discouragement. The rewards of work well done will be worth the effort."[3]

The flypaper hung from the ceiling. I remember seeing the coiled, brown sticky paper hanging in the house. Evidently an odor wafted from it that appeared attractive to the common housefly. Several days after hanging the paper, many of these insects would be stuck fast. It appeared an effective and safe approach to eliminating the pesky nuisances from our homes and porches.

Although I don't recommend flypaper to cause us to "stick to it," flypaper may be the only reliable method used in getting some individuals to complete a task. Procrastination, excuses, and delays prevent them and others from ever seeing the finished product. The waste of precious time faces all those with whom this person must work.

Christ, our Bridegroom, desires to aid us in our attempts to fulfill the tasks given to us, even the procrastinators. And that driving energy, when called upon, will not only supply the strength we need, but reveal the wonders of completed work done for Him.

One of the greatest gifts I can give myself is that of completing a task. As I recognize the diligence He has given, I assert my focus and my energies to the task at hand. Resolved to finish it for Him, I find joy in my efforts.

I have learned that my first step in being a truly diligent worker is to seek His face first every morning. Before I even arise from bed, I pray two prayers. The first is *Set a guard over my mouth, O Lord; keep watch over the door of my lips* (Psalm 141:3). Knowing I possess "foot-in-mouth-disease," I have learned the power of this prayer. Since my goal is to have only words that reflect His love to pass my lips, I trust Him to filter through the negative words that may flow past them, and to stop the ones that hurt and hinder His ministry.

My second prayer is "Lord, prepare me for all the tasks You have chosen for me this day. Anoint me with Your Spirit as I surrender to You and Your will. May Christ be ever before me. Amen." While the wording may be different on different days because of the events forthcoming, nonetheless I recognize His presence and trust in His strength.

Tasks accomplished for Him are supplied with diligence from Him. Although desiring to delay some of the more unpleasant assignments (like cleaning the toilets), I eventually commit myself to finishing them. And Christ promises that, when my strength rests in Him with power through His Spirit in my inner being, I will be able to do *immeasurably more than* (I) *could possibly ask or imagine – according to His power that is at work within* (me) (Ephesians 3:16-20).

Whether raising children for Him, whether working in a factory or classroom, whether speaking and writing, whether caring for a sick husband, He supplies the diligence needed. Focused on the eternal love of the Risen Christ, I move forward with dogged determination. His tasks for me are worthy of completion. What greater gift could I give Him in return for all He has done for me!

Chapter 2

COMPASSION

However difficult the circumstances had been in her life before, the depths of grief now swallowed her inside. No one expected his death. Loved by so many, she couldn't imagine the end result. Yet, after many days of illness, he died. And where was Jesus? Why hadn't He come sooner? Anguish and confusion filled Mary and Martha as they tried to comprehend the permanent removal of their dearly beloved brother.

"He's calling for you, Mary," she heard Martha say. "Go to Him."

Rushing past the other mourners, she ran down the street to meet Him. Falling at His feet, she wept and cried, "Lord, if you had been here, my brother would not have died" (John 11:32).

Moved deeply in His heart with compassion, Jesus could not contain the grief He felt. Although assured and confident of Lazarus' upcoming resurrection, Jesus still experienced intense sorrow for Mary and those nearby. Groans of anguish surfaced as if coming from the very depths of His inner being. Entering into the sorrow of Mary, He could not hide the pain. The reality of death struck Him with great force.

Gentle silence followed, as tears began to stream down His cheeks. He wept for those left behind. The sorrow was almost more than He could bear.

Just as Jesus entered into the sorrow of Mary and Martha, so He continues to enter into our grief. He rests deeply within our spirit on a daily basis to assure us of His comfort, His love and especially His compassion.

While fingers point heavenward and cry, "Why did you do this, Lord?" He weeps uncontrollably. His eyes shed tears on our behalf for He *does not willingly bring affliction or grief on the children of men* (Lamentations 3:33). His heart cannot bear the pain and inner anguish that occurs. With compassion that far exceed our own, He draws into our circumstances, our hearts and our lives, to restore and revive us. Just when we feel we cannot bear it any longer, He emerges as the power source we need.

He never wants us to go it alone – He offers His strength. He aches over decisions that are made and events that happen that turn our hearts cold. Rather He hopes they will restore us unto Him. He desires faith and trust in the midst of the storm, and knows that when it falters, He will provide the faith we lack – if only we keep our eyes on Him. When pounded on all sides with crisis, death, evil and despair, He aches and cries and pleads for us to fix our eyes on Him – not necessarily to remove the circumstances but to guide us *through the valley of the shadow of death* (Psalm 23:4).

The compassion of our God go deeper than any person can imagine. While others show compassion, few experience the depth of sorrow He feels and continues to feel. He grieves, He cries, He comforts – to save and to bring about a healing beyond comprehension. As the mountains crumble, as the seas roar, as the water floods over our spirits, His Spirit takes over and supplies all we need. His eternal compassion never cease and are forever before us and beside us.

Because of the Lord's great love, we are not consumed, for his compassion never fail. They are new every morning; great is your faithfulness (Lamentations 3:22-23).

Intertwined

With roses the size of platters, all who viewed them stood in awe. The colors glowed and the blending of hues and shades amazed everyone. No garden ever looked more beautiful. But early one morning, the owner became bewildered with a new, rather hidden, discovery in his garden. Amidst the roses, another vine of rare and unusual beauty grew. Because of its unexpected, yet beautiful appearance, the owner refused to remove it until sure of its impact on the roses. In time, he discovered that, rather than choking and destroying the roses, it enhanced their beauty. Intertwined between and among them, the vine added a glistening array of water droplets that spilled onto the roses. Accepting the new addition as an unseen blessing, the gardener rejoiced at its intrusion and even sensed comfort from its presence. While remaining almost unseen to the observer, it illuminated and highlighted the already stunning beauty of the roses.

As love from the Bridegroom pronounces itself to us in striking and profound ways, others watch in awe as He creates in us vessels of beauty. The love He generates through His Spirit emerges and flows into the lives of others. As the observers see the fruit of the Spirit, the deeds of righteousness, and the power of love, they marvel at the beautiful garden growing within. Yet unseen to them, another vine intertwines with love. As trials, sorrows and pain pounce on the bride, a precious gift is sent from the Bridegroom that none could possibly see or understand except through the tears that spill on the roses. Touching her heart with a deep, inner compassion, He floods comfort into her spirit in the midst of the pain. Never exposed before, even the bride had not noticed its presence. Yet when experiencing its effect, she aches and yearns for continued intertwining with its love.

Although love is commonly accepted as coming from Christ, few seldom understand or visualize the intertwined presence of compassion. Except in extremely excruciating circumstances, its presence goes unnoticed. Yet Christ, in His depth of love for us, enters our sorrows and shares our grief. He cannot separate the gift of love from the gift of compassion.

Overshadowed by pain, we often cry for relief. His sense of love soothes the hurts and absorbs the pain. Yet we cannot imagine the tears He sheds for us at the eternal throne of His Father. Pleading for us, He asks that the blows we encounter be as gentle as possible. He cries. His Spirit groans for us as we plead to Him. That compassion –

that grief – then comforts us. Surrounded with a host of angels, singing praises of joy for our growth in Him, the Bridegroom then soothes us with His eternal tears and everlasting love. His only purpose for the pain: to add tears of compassion to the roses of love sprouting in our hearts. In the process, He creates a more glorious likeness of Him. What greater glory could there be!

Praise the Lord, O my soul; all my inmost being, praise his holy name. Praise, the Lord, O my soul, and forget not all his benefits...who redeems your life from the pit and crowns you with love and compassion, who satisfies your desires with good things so that your youth is renewed like the eagle's (Psalm 103:1-2,4-5).

The Crown

He crowns you with love and compassion (Psalm 103:4).

The intertwined crown rested on His head. While most kings wear crowns of precious jewels and priceless gold, His consisted of long, sharp thorns. Placing it on His head only served as a tool with which to mock Him. And the pain did not end with its placement. Using a staff, the soldiers added to the misery by continually striking Him on the head again and again. Humiliation only proved the seed for their attempts to torture Him. The continuing pain was the desired outcome. Filled with undeserved hatred, they relished debasing and lowering Him as the worst of criminals.

Yet the Bridegroom could have walked away. He could have pronounced eternal judgment on all present. A legion of angels awaited His call – only to hear none. Why? Why wear the humiliation and disgrace of an intertwined crown? The answer – love and compassion! His love overflowed beyond human understanding. His tender compassion for a people without a shepherd surfaced. They needed this Bridegroom, this Shepherd in their lives. Without Him, His bride would never see the heavenly home He prepared for them. Without His expansive love and compassion, the eternal rewards of forgiveness and power and faith would never be theirs. He knew that. His love accepted the crown and cross for love's sake. The intertwined crown, worn to the cross, fulfilled the needed requirements. Now the bride is His – to share that love – to administer that compassion to others.

Be Like-Minded

The story is told of a mentally impaired child whose parents took him to a local drugstore. Before long, he was found playing with some of the bottles taken from the shelves. Disgruntled with his behavior, the druggist ordered him to put the bottles back. When no response came back, he then scolded him for his behavior. In short order, his little sister approached him, put her arms around his neck and whispered something in his ear. Without any further hesitation, the little boy placed the bottles back on the shelves. Amazed at the results, the druggist asked the sister why her approach worked and not his. Her response – "You see," his sister explained, "he doesn't understand when you talk to him like that. I just love it into him."[4]

Oh, that we would learn this art of compassion. When encountering individuals who react unlovingly during stressful, difficult times – just love it into them. As they struggle and fuss and fume over heartbreaking circumstances, creating uncomfortable working conditions or adverse actions at home – just love it into them. When driven by loneliness or internal dissatisfaction, needing confirmation and positive strokes – just love it into them.

On these occasions, we must turn to the Bridegroom and seek the gift of compassion intertwined with love. Never seeking our own justification or our own self-will, we seek His will and His strength to "love it into them." As the love flows through the Savior, so does the compassion – they cannot be disconnected – for God is a God of love and compassion. As He lovingly pours that compassion into us, we cannot help but provide that same compassion to others.

The Lord is gracious and compassionate, slow to anger and rich in love. The Lord is good to all; he has compassion on all he has made (Psalm 145:8-9).

"*Though the mountains be shaken and the hills be removed, yet my unfailing love for you will not be shaken nor my covenant of peace removed," says the Lord, who has compassion on you* (Isaiah 54:10).

Yet the Lord longs to be gracious to you; He rises to show you compassion. For the Lord is a God of justice. Blessed are all who wait for Him (Isaiah 30:18).

As we wait for the love and compassion from the Bridegroom, He rewards us with love and compassion to offer to others. No matter how difficult, no matter how challenging. He will receive the victory in your life. He will supply you with all the compassion and love you need.

Therefore, as God's chosen people, holy and dearly loved, clothe yourselves with compassion, kindness, humility, gentleness and patience (Col. 3:12).

Praise the Lord. Blessed is the man who fears the Lord, who finds great delight in his commands...Even in darkness light dawns for the upright, for the gracious and compassionate and righteous man (Psalm 112:1,4).

Chapter 3

A STRONG WORK ETHIC

The grime under her fingernails affected her little. The blackened hands, reminders of the soot that had recently covered much of her lovely home, mattered little. She only glowed from within and without over the transformation incurred through her many hours of labor.

The oil-burning stove exploded overnight. Soot and ash from the pipes spilled into the entire room. While sickened at the result, this precious woman never hesitated to attack the task at hand. No complaint crossed her mouth. Only singing – eternal singing.

"Things happen," she said. "It will be easy to fix and only hard work is involved. I can do it. I will complete my task sent from heaven today."

On the days that followed, her mind discovered new ways to decorate. New challenges for repair and replacement spurred her creative juices. The room, though tarnished for a time, eventually appeared renewed and revitalized. The end result brought the joy of accomplishment and peace in a job well done.

Tasks, labors, jobs – often tedious, boring and monotonous. Yet when seen through the eyes of another, a special Lover and Bridegroom, our tasks take on new vision and new hope. Accepting the responsibility at hand, a joyful spirit invades, and the desire for His quality and beauty slips into our minds. Looking heavenward, we rely on the power of the Spirit to open our eyes to the positive thoughts rather than dwell on the negative. Sensing the love of that Bridegroom, even in the midst of the grime and soot and ash, we are warmed by the glow of His presence. Questioning how we achieved so much with so little, we praise Him for the wonders He supplied.

All too many of us become swallowed up in the routine. Desiring to accomplish much on our own, we feel defeated and disenchanted with our goals. Seeking to earn a large income, working hard to impress others or striving to be the best, we forget that, apart from our Bridegroom, little satisfaction in our inner being will occur. Temporary happiness may elude us into thinking we can go it alone. But eventually, another task must be sought and more time spent in bringing about that happiness again.

But the power of the Spirit and the love of Jesus Christ grant us a productive, industrious spirit, simply for the asking. Desiring to feed us with a strong work ethic, He submerges our failures and elevates His energy. Whether caring for a parent, washing the dishes after a well-planned meal, changing the baby's diapers, teaching a classroom of children, working in the executive realm, or struggling with the monotony of factory work, His love floods our souls. He opens doors that lead to accomplished tasks and nudges us to share His love with others. No task is too small – no accomplishment too great. His tender, loving arms shield, protect and guide us through the challenges and tasks at hand. Our expanded purpose of life flows out to others as they see the joy that can only come in and through Him.

Seek Him For The Vision

To many women, a vision for life appears obscure and impossible. Rather than seeking a vision for ministry, they hide behind excuses, such as, "I'm too fat." "I'm not pretty enough." "I have so few gifts and talents." "I wouldn't know where to begin." "I really don't want a vision. It may require too much work."

Excuses sadden our Savior of Eternal Love. He died to free us from the constricting bands that hold us back in our labors for Him. A ministry for His bride is established and planned. Yet excuses stand in the way. Laziness or fear draws us back from a planned goal. They lie dead in the water, rather than float on the surface of His love. They never sail beyond our fearful, lazy hearts, and the exciting, generating results never emerge or sail forward.

We must step past the excuses. Falling on our knees before the Bridegroom, we need only request direction and commit our will and ways into His hands. Secure in His promises of supply, we rest in His love until that direction and supply are awarded. It may not – in fact, probably will not – happen overnight. Many times we must be groomed for the job. The study of His Word, given to us for growth, must occur. Events may need to test our sincerity and to spur on our love for Him. Then when the excuses are gone and the trust level is at His needed point, the vision becomes clear and the results astound us.

Some of us may already be living the vision and not even recognize it. While praying for a dynamic ministry in prayer, yet seeing nothing occur on a grand scale, we assume the vision is not met. All the while, Jesus pleads with us to practice intercessory prayer, praise Him for His goodness in the wait and rejoice in the small events accomplished that day. Seeking His power and goodness is sufficient for each day for just as the Israelites received "just enough" manna for each day in the wilderness, so that same love is "just enough" for us as we live one day at a time for Him (Exodus 16:17-18).

Rather than look for the grandiose, look for Christ. Seek His face. The vision will flow through Him into you and the fulfillment of that vision will be visible one day at a time. In the process, you will grow to understand that there is no greater vision in your life than to know and love your precious Bridegroom.

Trust Him For The Strength

A vision takes many forms and shapes. I cannot determine your vision and you cannot determine mine. Each must discover that vision by seeking the power of Christ. Once the vision is established, doubt and misgivings may pour in. Concerned about supply, we throw in the towel before climbing onto the mat. Failing to trust the Bridegroom for the supply, we withdraw and then blame Him for not following through on His end of the bargain.

Yet He assures us – *You are God's workmanship, created in Christ*

Jesus to do good works, which God prepared in advance for us to do (Ephesians 2:10). He lays out a map of what He desires that we achieve and provides the strength and resources to do so. He cries out, "Tell yourself this important fact: *I can do everything through him who gives me strength* (Philippians 4:13). I will provide every minute detail and physical need necessary to accomplish that task. It is promised. Trust Me!"

Are there risks involved? Possibly. Will it be easy? Not always. What if I fail in my attempts? You may, but He lovingly forgives and opens other doors to continue in your vision. Grow through each step. Pray for the Spirit's strength and wisdom. It will be provided – one day at a time.

Exhaustion may occur. When it does, pray for guidance in relieving that exhaustion. Perhaps our labors are dependent on acceptance of others, at the cost of our own health and our family's well-being. Maybe the task at hand is taken in steps too large for us. Or, in the midst of the exhaustion, there may be cause to rejoice in the amazing work done for Him. But always, take time to rest in Him and trust that our strength will eventually be restored through His abundant love.

Our Bridegroom never said the way would be easy. In fact He said, *In this world you will have trouble. But take heart! I have overcome the world* (John 16:33b). Also in His parable of the sower and the seed as told in Luke 8:4-15, He shares the following regarding the seed sown on good soil: *It came up and yielded a crop, a hundred times more than was sown...But the seed on good soil stands for those with a noble and good heart, who hear the word, retain it, and by persevering produce a crop* (vs. 8,15).

The seed is sown. Moved by the Holy Spirit to accept that seed, it takes root and becomes established through the constant nourishment of God's Word. Embracing it deeply in our heart and soul, that seed sprouts and yields a crop through hard work and a loving attitude. Leaning on the power of Christ in our lives we willingly produce that crop – a hundred times more than was sown. Not because *we* did it, but because our precious Bridegroom moved quietly and gently in us through His Spirit. He planted the seed. His Spirit moved us to accept it, by our acknowledgment to willingly hear and listen. As Christ produces the harvest, others learn to recognize His power and yearn for that same comfort, power and love found only in Him. How wonderful to be used by Him!

Take Pride In His Work

When it snows, she has no fear of her household; for all are clothed in scarlet. She makes coverings for her bed; she is clothed in fine linen and purple. Her husband is respected at the city gate, where he takes his seat among the elders of the land. She makes linen garments and sells them and supplies the merchants with sashes (Proverbs 31:21-24). And why? Because she is a woman who fears the Lord.

There you go again, Jan, throwing up that perfect woman! I can't live up to that. It is too impossible, so why try?

An attitude buried in this thinking stifles the seed as soon as the Bridegroom plants it. In reality you are depending on self, rather than on the One whose source of strength will supply all your need. He will not give you a vision you cannot ultimately fulfill by His power. He proposes His plan to you. He pleads with you to trust Him – to rest in His strength. He yearns for you to know and surrender to His call of service and to build, through His Spirit, the strong work ethic He desires for you.

If you cannot speak in front of large groups, then teach a women's Bible class. If you cannot teach a women's Bible class, then teach small children in Sunday school. If you cannot teach at all, serve others through mercy, caring and compassion.

Pray for Jesus to reveal His will for you today. Accept the daily circumstances and situations as part of that will (even it wasn't on your planned agenda) and work wholeheartedly to complete and fulfill it. God's vision for you may be in the future, taking baby steps each day to reach its full height. Or His vision for you may be a daily trust in serving those around you. Or He may ask you to share His love light in dramatic ways. But whatever His choice, accept His vision as yours. Then praise Him for the goodness, power and love of His Spirit to achieve it.

Joy in the overwhelming assurance, comfort, strength and supply of Christ fills our being, for we recognize His tender touch. As the days bring about hard work and service for Him, appreciation floods our souls. Realizing our weaknesses and acknowledging His goodness strengthens our vision and increases a strong work ethic. Looking at His embraceable love through His Word and prayer, we praise Him for the awesome gift of a job well done.

Chapter 4

WISDOM

Buried deep within her came the cry for help. She knew she needed Him. His presence seemed to have faded and she could not understand why. Was it something she had done or did He just choose to leave her helpless? "Dear Jesus," she begged. "Help me understand where I am to turn. Why have you deserted me?"

She lay prostrate on the floor, agonizing. Desiring a touch of Him, she closed her eyes and listened. Then a verse entered her thoughts, Trust in the Lord with all your heart and lean not on your own understanding; in all your ways acknowledge him, and he will make your paths straight (Proverbs 3:5,6). Looking heavenward, she remembered moments of His presence in the past. Never leaving her without hope before, she said, "Jesus, You promised that You would not leave me comfortless. I am claiming that promise. Even though I do not understand this chaos I am going through, I will trust You. You are my precious Bridegroom and I believe You will make my paths straight. Give me the strength and wisdom to believe and receive that truth."

While the sorrow did not leave for some time, each day elevated her to a new height of Christ's love. She prayed for the Holy Spirit's strength and guidance in searching the Scriptures. Trusting Him to enable her to become wise unto salvation, she rested in His loving arms. Each prayer brought her closer to the Lover of her soul and a ravenous hunger for His Word split the sorrow into joy and peace. To her, the Word opened doors of power and the quiet time alone soothed her floundering spirit. Desiring to be like Christ, she prayed earnestly, "Jesus, give me Your wisdom. Give me Your understanding so that I may see and understand and believe. Praise You, for I know it is already happening. Thank You, Jesus."

In the trials and tragedies of life, we often cry out for just a glimpse of understanding. When it makes no sense, when the pain doesn't go away, when a loved one dies in spite of our efforts, when a baby is prematurely claimed, when family division stares us in the face, when persecution pounds at the fiber of our beliefs – we cry, "Help me understand. Give me hope."

Although absorbed in His Word, callused from bended knee, and smothered with words of well-wishers, our spirits still question the workings of God. "When will it all end? How much longer, Lord? I just can't take it any longer," we cry. "Where are You, Jesus? Why do you feel so far away?"

Yet in due time, we slowly begin to understand. Scanning the pages of Peter's first letter, we read, *And the God of all grace, who called you to his eternal glory in Christ, after you have suffered a little while, will himself restore you and make you strong, firm and steadfast* (1 Peter 5:10). Christ, our Lover, touches our heart with His Spirit and says, "In My eternal plan of things, I will strengthen you. But you must grow to love Me first. You must desire My wisdom and My strength and My understanding above all the treasures of heaven. When that occurs, the windows of heaven will open and the floodgates of My power will embrace you. While you are still searching, I will still be there. I will hold your hand and cry with you. Trust Me. I love you."

Pleasant To Your Soul

The image of her loving Shepherd flooded her mind and spirit. Her search was not in vain. New droplets of information sprinkled into her life – first like a light mist, then slowly increasing into a heightened revelation of a warm summer shower. The washing over her soul cleansed the hurt, the pain and the grief. In its place, new life burst forth as flowers exploding with beauty and vibrancy. In her search for wisdom, she found Christ. In her calling out for insight and her crying aloud for understanding, she discovered that deep love she desired and craved many months before. Like a bubbling brook flowing over the rocks in her life, the vision and view of Christ's presence in her life glistened in her spirit. "He is my wisdom. He is my power. He is my strength," she whispers. "It is all right to experience despair and loneliness and to feel helpless. For in that process, I sought Him and found Him. I now love Him with all my heart and soul. What joy He brings. Thank You, Jesus."

Daily we encounter mini and maxi trials. Daily we need Him. Daily we must seek Him. Arising in the morning, our hearts need to turn heavenward as we say, "Dearest Jesus, give me Your wisdom today. Help me in my search for You. Only then can I serve others through You and in You. Help me to *look for it as silver and search for it as for hidden treasure, then (I) will understand the fear of the Lord and find the knowledge of God. For (You) give wisdom, and from (Your) mouth comes knowledge and understanding* (Proverbs 2:4-6, parenthesis added). In You, Jesus, only in You."

When we acknowledge His power and love and presence in our lives, He supplies a view into His kingdom. Through continued Spirit-led study of His Word and through the trials and chaotic circumstances in our lives, His wisdom and understanding replace ours. As we yield to Him, His Spirit overwhelms us, motivates us, and strengthens us. While we cannot comprehend how it is done, we feel its effects. As the gentle breezes of His goodness blow into our lives, a love for our precious Bridegroom deepens. None can compare. None can replace it, for He stills and quiets our soul.

More Precious Than Gold

The mine twisted and turned beneath the ground. Veins of rich gold glistened when exposed to the light. She was rich. She knew she could possess almost anything she desired. Yet the more she bought, the more she wanted to buy. No matter how many houses, cars, and planes she owned, a nagging void chewed away at her inside. If she had everything money could buy, why wasn't she happy?

The farmer had an amazing crop that year. With his granaries filled and his silos overflowing, he marveled as his accomplishment.

Swelled with pride, he determined to build bigger and better barns to hold it all. Yet that night he died. (Luke 12:16-21)

The possessions, the pride – what value did they truly hold? With nothing stored up for eternity, they only existed. All was lost eventually.

The wisdom of God glows and grows. It holds the secrets of heaven. It reveals the power and love of an awesome God. It manifests itself in the person of Jesus Christ. It is revealed in the ultimate of love on the cross and through His resurrection. And as the nail-scarred hands reach out to us, He takes us to the heights to view Him as He is. For *blessed is the (woman) who finds wisdom, the (woman) who gains understanding, for (wisdom) is more profitable than silver and yields better returns than gold. (Wisdom) is more precious than rubies, nothing you desire can compare with her. Long life is in her hand; in her left hand are riches and honor. (Wisdom's) ways are pleasant ways, and all her paths are peace. (Wisdom) is a tree of life to those who embrace her; those who lay hold of her will be blessed* (Proverbs 3:13-18, parenthesis added).

But do people know where to find wisdom? Where can they find understanding? No one knows where to find it, for it is not found among the living. "It is not here," says the ocean. "Nor is it here," says the sea. It cannot be bought for gold or silver. Its value is greater than all of the gold of Ophir, greater than precious onyx stone or sapphires. Wisdom is far more valuable than gold and crystal. It cannot be purchased with jewels mounted in fine gold. Coral and valuable rock crystal are worthless in trying to get it. The price of wisdom is far above pearls. Topaz from Ethiopia cannot be exchanged for it. Its value is greater than the purest gold. But do people know where to find wisdom? Where can they find understanding? For it is hidden from the eyes of all humanity. Even the sharp-eyed birds in the sky cannot discover it. But Destruction and Death say, "We have heard a rumor of where wisdom can be found." God surely knows where it can be found, for he looks throughout the whole earth, under all the heavens. He made the winds blow and determined how much rain should fall. He made the laws of the rain and prepared a path for the lightning. Then, when he had done all this, he saw wisdom and measured it. He established it and examined it thoroughly. And this is what he says to all humanity: "The fear of the Lord is true wisdom; to forsake evil is true understanding" (Job 28:12-28, New Living Translation).

Be A Woman Of Wisdom

The heart of Jesus Christ desires that we recognize the spirit of His wisdom within each and every one of us. Alone, we cannot be the vessels that radiate His love to others. With Him, the bride can be *clothed in strength and dignity; she can laugh at the days to come. She speaks with wisdom, and faithful instruction is on her tongue* (Proverbs 31:25-26). Through Christ, she can *spread everywhere the fragrance of the knowledge of him* (2 Corinthians 2:14).

Yet too often we shudder in our boots rather than fall down on our knees when the need for wisdom and strength arises. Presented with difficult people, opportunities to witness, denying oneself, or sacrificing our bodies as living sacrifices, we doubt that the wisdom from Christ pertains to us at that moment in time. Our selfishness surfaces and we shout, "But what about me? Don't my needs matter?"

And Jesus answers, "Only in Me does anything matter. Only in denying self and taking up your cross can My wisdom flow into and through you. It doesn't make sense and it never will. *For my thoughts are not your thoughts, neither are your ways my ways...As the heavens are higher than the earth, so are my ways higher than your ways and my thoughts than your thoughts*" (Isaiah 55:8,9).

But He promises a flood of spiritual blessings in the inner places, where it really matters. As we take confidence in His wisdom in our lives, we succumb to a realization that everything in our life has a divine, eternal purpose. All events, every timetable, each happening, yielded to Him is in His full control. While we may not comprehend the powerfully love-filled purpose for the events in our lives, we do learn to acknowledge Him as our Lord and Savior. We accept the lessons, the scraping, the abrasions with praise instead of grumbling. His wisdom reveals a love greater than any known before – an unconditional love that always desires our best interest and provides a healthy spirit open to His goodness, power and strength.

There is no wisdom greater than Christ Jesus Himself. Seek Him daily. Pray for the Wisdom that fills the spirit and floods the soul. *And the peace of God, which transcends all understanding, will guard your hearts and your minds in Christ Jesus* (Philippians 4:7).

Chapter 5

RADIANCE

The open field attracted them. Sparkling lights exploded continuously. I marveled at the brilliance displayed throughout the waving grain. The electric display of the lightning bugs filled my soul and enabled me to catch but a slight vision of the power of many working together. "Lord," I cried. "Now I understand why Christians need each other. Alone, our light is but one flicker among a dark world. But together, we create a luminous display of Your glory. May this picture forever be in my heart and soul."

God's radiance spills into our lives quite unexpectedly. We can't see it. We don't feel it. We aren't even aware of its presence. Because the power of Christ rests in our inner being, His radiance springs into our lives. It is in and through Him that the gospel light emerges. As we recognize and accept our own weaknesses and acknowledge His strengths, His light and His glory issue through us to others. It is not to our credit, but to His. Alone, we reflect humanity. In Him, we reflect radiance detectable to all with whom we come in contact.

In difficult times, I remember often quoting the verse, *Those who look to him are radiant; their faces are never covered with shame* (Psalm 34:5). Awed by His love and powerful light in my life, I prayed, "Dearest Jesus, please may all those with whom I come in contact today, not see me, but only You and Your radiance." Recognizing the tender touches of His goodness in my life, I wanted the power and love of Jesus Christ to be evident. I craved within my spirit to elevate Him and worship Him with my very life. Knowing that in Him, I could not be put to shame, I walked (and sometimes plodded) through each day secure that He came first. Only in His divine presence could that take place.

He Knew Him As A Friend

He spent many hours in His presence. Whether on the mountain top or in the special tent of meeting, Moses maintained a unique and special relationship with the divine God. Speaking with Him one-on-one, he shared a relationship beyond comprehension. Moses prayed to, honored and praised the loving God with whom he shared a friendship.

And gutsy – man, was he gutsy! "Now, show me Your glory," he requested. Speaking to the Triune God, he had the courage and audacity to ask for a personal viewing of His divine presence. Yet God had said, "No man can see God's face and live." Wasn't he afraid? Wasn't he concerned about the consequences?

In spite of this bold request, God, the Maker of the earth, promised to honor his request. He said, "I am pleased with you and I know you by name." Yet there were restrictions. Only a portion of His glory could be viewed. To allow Moses the privilege of viewing His goodness, He shielded him by placing him in the cleft of a rock and covered his face with His own almighty hand. Having passed, He removed His hand and allowed Moses to witness His back. Absorbing the Divine's radiance, Moses then carried that brilliance down into the camp.

Standing before the Lord's people, fear enveloped them. How could they come near to the one who radiated the presence of the Almighty God? They desired to hear and heed the commands given to this dynamic, yet humble man, but feared the outcome of drawing too close. Understanding their fears, Moses placed a veil over his face to cover his radiance before speaking to them.

Upon every entrance into the tent of meeting, Moses removed the veil to allow free access with His Friend and Savior. And after every communication with the presence of God, Moses reflected that radiance, for God existed in his own heart and soul as well.

With the veil again covering his face, he returned to the people and gave them God's messages of power and love. While the radiance was hidden from the people, his unique relationship with an Almighty God was not (Exodus 33:12-23, 34:29-35).

God's people today continue to reflect that glory. Communication with the Father, renewal through the Spirit, and empowerment through Jesus, the Rock cleft for us, we radiate the power, love and light of the Almighty God. And we do not have to stand in the cleft of a rock to see the goodness of God. He exists within our very being. He activates, motivates, and energizes us. He works better than the Energizer Bunny! He will keep going and going and going …long after all batteries, all events, all circumstances, all lives end. He is present within us. He is here and now for Scripture says, *These things are written that you may believe that Jesus is the Christ, the Son of God, and that by believing you may have life in his name* (John 20:31). *Now this is eternal life: that they may know you, the only true God, and Jesus Christ, whom you have sent* (John 17:3). His eternal presence is for us today. His light floods our depleted souls and radiates forth to others. When we are weak, He is strong. We can say with confidence, " We will look to Him and be radiant and our faces will never be covered with shame" for He supplies all we lack.

He Increases As We Decrease

Ouch! That painful thought of self-denial again. The thought of dying to self, of taking up a cross for Him, seems more than I can bear. I prefer having the control. I relish being in charge. I don't want anyone to dictate where I go and with whom I choose to associate. I like making my own choices and am willing to pay the price.

Yet the price often costs more than we imagined and the consequences are overbearing. Wondering how God could have allowed us to get into these messes, we fail to realize that our own self-choosing opened the doors for many of the messes afflicting us. Yet God gets the blame. He should have prevented bad from happening, enabling us to shine like stars – not for Him but for our own glory.

Our cherished Bridegroom does not work that way. He does not force Himself upon us. Rather, He desires that our wills yield to His

– that our cravings rest in the bosom of His kind and tender heart. While it is true that surrender is difficult and that yielding control to His compassionate hands is a daily struggle, yet He waits with open arms to embrace us with all the goodness of His kingdom. The internal, spiritual, enlightened alterations within occur through Him in abundance – not to harm us but to emblazon us with unexplained peace, joy and light. There is no limit to what He can do in us, through us and for us when we give our very lives in service to Him. While the circumstance may be difficult (those nasty crosses), yet the eternal pleasures far surpass the troubles. In the midst of the storms, Jesus gives us the smile of joy that lightens the face and calms the troubled breast. The transformation of our soul removes the veil that covers our hearts for *only in Christ is it taken away* (2 Corinthians 3:14). Now *we, who with unveiled faces all reflect the Lord's glory, are being transformed into his likeness with ever-increasing glory, which comes from the Lord, who is the Spirit* (2 Corinthians 3:18).

Till Death Do Us Part

Her emaciated body appeared gaunt and limp. The bony shoulder blades protruded. The cancer was bad, and her treatments had taken its toll. Viewing her picture reminded me of someone in a concentration camp. The pain in my heart remains, as remembrances of that picture shadow the vibrant life I recalled from younger, better years. How could doctors allow her to become so depleted? Why would they not stop the treatment when viewing the horrible impact on her body? Why didn't they do more to replenish and restore her body in the process?

Questions – those unrelenting questions. Witnessing a loved one enduring the ravages of an illness cut at our very soul. Believing that an all-powerful, loving God is in control seems to elude us. Yet, His Word promises strength. His comfort is never further than clasped hands away. His promise of better days is only a breath away.

Her husband struggled day after day, encountering her bankruptcy of body. His questions surfaced. Knowing that her trust and hope rested securely in the risen Christ, his hope rested in the assurance that somehow God would sustain them both. But with doubt and guilt plaguing his spirit, he ached to see a revelation of the outcome of her faith.

As weeks waned into months and months into years, healing became less and less evident. Yet her faith refused to give up hope even in the most trying of times. While the pain and physical torture filled her every waking moment, yet her cries to the Lord continued. She accepted Christ as her safe harbor, her place of safety. She prayed for the strength to endure, for the patience of others, and for the love of those who worked with her.

Approaching the end of this life, her husband, two sons and a daughter-in-law viewed an amazing disclosure of Christ's kingdom in her life. In the midst of her constant fight for breath, their eyes witnessed an overwhelming look of peace and calmness on her face. Near death, her face reflected an indescribable radiance. Jesus, her Bridegroom, revealed He was there to take her home. What glory! What ecstasy! What a confirmation of His presence in her inner being! He had been there all the time. Now, with her work complete in this life, He wrapped her in His garment of light and carried her to the room prepared for her in heaven.

While the relationship of husband and wife brought separation, it will only be the twinkling of an eye for her. But her husband experiences with full force the marriage phrase, "till death do us part." The loneliness, the expanse of emptiness, the heartache and the grief follow. But the graphic joy of remembering her radiant death will forever soothe and calm his troubled heart. Her Bridegroom, Jesus Christ, came to get her. Of that he was certain.

Glowing before us is the knowledge that the death of Christ cancels the phrase, "till death us do part." Because of Christ Jesus' torturous redemption on a *cross of wood, our physical death only leads to life. While that life begins the moment we accept the Spirit's leading into faith, it continues as He draws us into Christ's presence. As we seek Him through His Word, through the strengthening resource in the Lord's supper, and through prayer, the supreme evidence of goodness spills out through us as little gospel lights that shine out to others. And it culminates in eternity as our earthly bodies die and decay.*

But nothing can separate us from the love of Christ – not even death. For death is the open door to the heavenly realms and Christ, our Bridegroom, is the Key. And one day He will gather all His glowing lights, like fireflies, into His kingdom to enjoy the marriage feast together. Then the Light will not only fill our hearts and radiate from our faces but be an eternal presence, glowing forever.

Chapter 6

PURITY

Oh, the drudgery of carrying around the burden of knowing purity fails to be a part of my personality. No matter the circumstances, seldom do I believe a pure heart is involved. I desire to share the Gospel of Christ, but often to what end? For my own pat on the back and with the intent of saying, "Look what I did"? Lifting a helping hand – how seldom do I desire some word of appreciation, of thanks? Yet in doing so, I am expecting something in return. A heart of true purity would not care, for His love motivates. His love is enough.

O, wretched person that I am! Who will save me from this humanness of desires and selfishness?

There are times when my heart aches to serve Him totally and completely. As my love for the Father and for Jesus Christ surges within, I perceive the closest touch of purity that one could experience. As fluent, prolific prayers flood from my mouth, I know that His presence is near. His purity wraps me in warmth. His gentle touch enables me to see, hear and feel His face. Purity – oh, yes, I experience purity – His purity.

No one asked her what she thought. No one cared. Her attitude toward others irritated like fingernails sliding down a chalkboard. The impact she left repulsed many. They forsook important events in their lives simply to avoid her endless chatter and selfish thinking. Her desire to have everything center on her and her desires created division, irritability and avoidance. Who would tell her? Who wanted to, for fear of her vain repercussions?

Unable to understand why others ignored her, she rationalized that they were the problem. "They are snobs. They are the selfish ones. They won't listen to me." Internalizing her anger and frustration, she stirred her boiling pot of damaged emotions even more. She never once asked God, "Am I doing something wrong? Is there something about me I need to change?" She found it so much easier to point the finger and allow her sores to fester.

Then one day, it happened. While trying to rationalize her position in the midst of her "friends," one finally retorted. "Will you please cease from forcing your ways and ideas on us? You perceive yourself as being the only one right and everyone else wrong. Take time to evaluate your own behavior. You need an overhaul."

Stunned and shocked, she retreated as a rabbit from a hungry fox. Her exit from the room could not be fast enough. Once in a secluded location, she fell to her knees and cried, "I don't understand. How can they be so cruel? What have I done that is so wrong?" Looking heavenward, she whispered, "Abba, Father, help me. If I need an overhaul, You must help me. I can't go on like this any more."

She heard nothing. She felt nothing. Yet in her soul, she knew the answer would come. Her need for the Father's approval created an ache, an ache that needed filling. Some way, somehow, He would reveal the open door of recovery.

Many precious women today cry out for understanding. Many believe that of and by themselves, they can acquire the overhaul desired. They read the right books, listen to the right tapes, watch the right videos, and speak with the right people, yet return home to the same old personality – sometimes controlling, sometimes angry, sometimes irritable. They cry, "What am I doing wrong? Where does the answer lie? Dear Jesus, I need your help!"

The Bridegroom hears our cry. He bends down with His nail-scarred hands and picks us up off the dirty floors of our lives and begins brushing off the crusty scabs and cleaning the open wounds that have accumulated. Neither too quickly nor too slowly but at a pace which only we can fathom and endure. Being touched by our cravings, He holds us gently to His breast and snuggles us closely, just as a shepherd with a floundering, lost lamb. Compassion reflects itself in tears that stream down His cheeks. It hurts Him so to see us in pain but He knows from His own experience that obedience is learned through pain. Remembering His own rejection of the Father, He now consoles us in our pain, assuring us that He will never reject us. He loves us beyond measure. He forgives eternally. He opens His heart and offers us one more thing – His purity.

Though soiled with negative attitudes, petty thoughts, selfish ambitions, angry reactions, Jesus points to us and said, "You are pure. Be clean." He touches us with grace and imparts His righteousness to us. For *God made him who had no sin to be sin for us, so that in him we might become the righteousness of God* (2 Corinthians 5:21). No matter the condition of our hearts, our bodies, or our spirits, He cleanses us and washes us clean, pure and holy in His eyes. Therefore, *let us draw near to God with a sincere heart in full assurance of faith, having our hearts sprinkled to cleanse us from a guilty conscience and having our bodies washed with pure water. Let us hold unswervingly to the hope we profess, for he who promised is faithful* (Hebrews 10:22-23).

A Godly Jealousy

Her envy startled everyone. No one comprehended the immense reaction Jackie would have to her sister's popularity. As the fame of her favored sister expanded, the anger inside Jackie became hotter. Not only reflecting feelings of inadequacy but of increasing rage, many feared for the restoration of their relationship. Thankfulness failed to exist in Jackie's inner being and an understanding of her sister's impact on others mattered little.

How could anyone help her? Observing the divide between them cut into the heart and soul of those who loved them. Yet nothing seemed to resolve the separation forming. Her jealously for the wrong things hardened her once loving heart and built a wall of incomprehensible thickness. Only a miracle could submerge the angry, hostile feelings and permit feelings of love and encouragement to take its place. How all their friends and relatives prayed for that miracle!

Sitting on the bottom of her pit of despair, she wondered, contemplated and evaluated her circumstances. Why had her hostility become so pronounced? What in her thinking had snapped and allowed this change in personality to overtake her once loving soul?

Opening the Bible, she discovered a verse that seemed to leap off the printed page: I am jealous for you with a godly jealousy. I promised you to one husband, to Christ, so that I might present you as a pure virgin to Him (2 Corinthians 11:2). As her shoulders began to tremble, she sensed a stab of deep conviction within her. How could she have been so utterly selfish?

Desperately desiring to be made right again with God, she fell to her knees and cried, "Father, please forgive me. Jealousy has overtaken my heart. Rather than rejoicing over the powerful impact that Marcy is making on the lives of others, I have only been mourning over my own cravings. I have anything but a godly jealousy. My heart and eyes have turned green with envy rather than white with pure joy. Help me to keep my eyes focused on my Bridegroom, Jesus, who alone can cleanse me and create the purity of heart I desire. Thank you for revealing my pride. Please clean me with hyssop, that I may be clean. Wash me, that I may be whiter than snow."

In our lives, jealousy abounds. Often our spirits are unaware of the deception until our own anger places us in pits of despair. In the depths of that pit, while some relish their self-pity and continue to languish in it, others recognize the need to turn to the God of all mercy and grace. For those whose hearts turn to the glory of God and seek His face, freedom from anger, jealousy and an unclean heart find total and complete relief.

With David, they cry out, *Create in me a pure heart, O God, and renew a steadfast spirit within me. Do not cast me from your presence or take your Holy Spirit from me. Restore to me the joy of your salvation and grant me a willing spirit, to sustain me* (Psalm 51:10-12).

As the *sacrifices of God are a broken spirit; a broken and contrite heart* (Psalm 51:17), His heart bends toward ours. Jesus Christ pours His blood sacrifice over our guilt and remembers it no more. Seeing no longer the sin-filled reactions of the past, He washes over us with a quiet spirit and a love-filled purity that only He can generate and produce. Enthralled by His abundant forgiveness, we yield our lives into His hands and pray for His loving Spirit to sustain us. Accepting the inability to do anything without the presence and power of Jesus Christ in our lives, we acknowledge that purity and holiness come only from Him. Rejoicing in His goodness, we proclaim His wonderful works and shout forth His praises. What an awesome God we have!

A Toothache

Sammy buried his head in his pillow. Mom said his toothache would not go away without a trip to the dentist. But Sammy knew that it meant shots, drilling and discomfort. He hated the thought and decided to proclaim that his toothache had disappeared. Yet within minutes of making that pronouncement, pain shot through his tooth and tears streamed down his cheeks.

Sensing his fears, his mother embraced him and assured him that the slight discomfort felt at the dentist paled in comparison to the pain he currently felt. Her tender touch and gentle words soothed his troubled heart, and although still apprehensive, he felt courage to move onward. "Anything," he thought, "anything to get rid of this pain."

As we swim in our own pools of inadequacies, fears, and frustrations, we pretend to be pure and humble. We pull every trick in the book and rationalize our way through every twist and turn, hoping to mask the deep, hidden lies. Yet the pain only seems to get worse. Knowing our hearts are not pure from conception, we despair of any hope of working it out on our own. After all, the need to be in control demands attention. God can't possibly work it out. It's all up to us.

Yet the pool gets deeper and the strength to continue stroking wanes. Our fingertips never touch the other side and before long, our "pure" intentions only pull us under. Finally, like a toothache that finds no relief, we reach toward the One who can restore our spirits and create new beings within.

We can't do it alone. Although we often ache to be pure in mind and spirit, we soon discover that we desire recognition, power or influence more. Professing to do it for the glory of God, we complain and whine when it didn't go our way. Standing back, we realize that no matter how deeply we desire pure motives, the toothache of impure motives surfaces. Who can save me from this? I desire to be pure and to have pure motives. So what happens?

Be reminded of Christ's words in John 15:4-5: *Remain in me, and I will remain in you. No branch can bear fruit by itself; it must remain in the vine. Neither can you bear fruit unless you remain in me. I am the vine; you are the branches. If a man remains in me and I in him, he will bear much fruit; apart from me you can do nothing.*

Left to our own devices, our own pride, our own self-imposed purity, we fail. The glow of our Bridegroom is veiled as our own desires for attention intercede. But as we fall in humble submission before His cross and acknowledge our desperate need for Him, His gifts of grace and mercy flow into our lives. Providing us with His purity, others see Him, not us. In spite of our errors, our foibles, and our foot-in-mouth disease, His gracious holiness floats to the surface and His strokes carry us to the other side. As we cry in despair, "I can't, Lord. But You can!" He takes over and erases our mistakes before the throne of grace. He can fix what is broken. He can fill what is empty. He can purify what is unclean. He can forgive and forgive and forgive. What amazing grace! Thank you, my precious Bridegroom!

And since we have a great priest over the house of God, let us draw near to God with a sincere heart in full assurance of faith, having our hearts sprinkled to cleanse us from a guilty conscience and having our bodies washed with pure water. Let us hold unswervingly to the hope we profess, for he who promised is faithful (Hebrews 10:21-23).

Chapter 7

REVERENCE

Buttons, bows and bangles glittered in the bright sunlight. The plain, ordinary little girl transformed before their very eyes. Once insignificant – now a celebrity. As her eyes sparkled, so did her soul. Never before had she experienced such a feeling of elation. Now accepted by others, she knew her life would change forever. Standing in awe of the person responsible for the makeover, she could not help but hug his leg and cry, "Thank you, thank you. You make me feel so special. How can I ever repay you?" With that the big man looked at her with eyes of pride and said, "You just did, my child. You just did."

In my life, I am very similar to that simple, transformed child. Feelings of being unwanted, unaccepted and unappreciated plummeted into my life more than once. While those in my family loved me, I still craved a sparkling soul. Little did I realize that it would take buttons, bows and bangles to change me from the inside out.

Buttons held my life together and kept me in my comfort zone. Yet when someone pushed my buttons or tried to unbutton my comfortable life, I rebelled and often engaged in a tug-of-war. Fear overcame and did a major job of overriding the possibilities of other options. I needed my abode of comfort. Buttoned in, I didn't want to be disturbed. Years later, I realized how a buttoned-up life confined me. In a step of faith, I opened my life to a new button, one surrendered to Christ and His love. That button of surrender filled me with spiritual joy and opened new vistas of courage, strength and wonder found only in Him. What excitement rushed into my soul when my button of surrender opened new visions of growth and ministry!

While a bow generally adorns a gift or beautifies a little girl's hair, my bow reflected insecurity. Being tall and skinny, wearing glasses bigger than my face, and lacking in the figure of most young ladies, my bow constricted me. It hindered my ability to see my physical self as anything but attractive. Hindered by these false assumptions of myself, I resorted to timidity and felt cheated because of my lack of lovely feminine features. But as the precious Savior, Jesus Christ, began to absorb my life and as my brokenness stripped me naked before him, I recognized the beauty He already beheld. Although the change in me revealed itself in outward ways, the Master's touch exposed a new beauty in my inward nature.

Oh, how I craved to have Him assure me of His acceptance! As I searched for the Bridegroom in His Word, His goodness spilled out into my lap. This tender Lover, who desired my best and wanted to tie all His blessings in a bow, created in me a beauty that would last into eternity. Being wrapped in His love, my insecurities of appearance and acceptance were tied with a scarlet ribbon no one could remove. Recognizing this scarlet ribbon as the blood that flowed though His veins, I glowed with His radiance.

A Christmas pin I possess is laden with sequins, beads and stars. What a glittering example of the greatest growth my soul embraced! As the sun, when shining on the pin, bounces with shimmering delight, I am reminded of the Son who sparkles my life with a vibrancy and security found nowhere else. Every sequin in life, though sometimes dull and mundane, reflects His glory. Even when the sparkle in my eyes is dulled due to grief, sorrow, heartache, or pain, His beads and bangles of comfort and joy return and remind me that in each day – every day, Christ is enough.

The spiritual joys of Jesus Christ, my Bridegroom, enhance my daily routines, my struggles and my ordinary life. His everyday miracles, often not evident before, now surface as the greatest revelation of His sparkling bangles in my life. From the rising of the sun to its setting thereof; from the laughter of a child to the hug of a little one who thinks you're the greatest ever; from the healing of a friend to the heavenly return of a loved one, the Bridegroom's sparkles of joy surface and amazingly radiate out to others.

As my strength flows from His glittering Spirit, I cannot help but lift up my eyes toward heaven and praise the Almighty God who changed my constricting buttons to buttons of surrender. As joy through my Bridegroom emerges, I rejoice in praise for His untying of the bows of insecurity and tying me with a scarlet ribbon of acceptance and unconditional love. As peace calms my troubled spirit and I sense an overpowering hunger and thirst for more of my Jesus, I exalt and extol the Father who sent His Son to allow His light to flow into me. Therein lies the shining response of a life filled with gratitude for One whose power flows within and creates a unique, special child. Without Him, I am lackluster. With Him, I sparkle.

The One To Be Revered

Sitting on the throne of grace, He looks down upon us in tender love. Viewing our grief, our pain, our floundering spirits, our Bridegroom remembers His gut-wrenching struggles in the Garden of Gethsemane. Even there, surrender exemplified His life. He loved His Father beyond comprehension and desired to accomplish His will, no matter how excruciating and painful the cost. In His prayers, He cried, *Father, I want those You have given Me to be with Me where I am, and to see My glory, the glory You have given Me because You love Me before the creation of the world. Righteous Father, though the world does not know You, I know You and they know that You have sent Me. I have made You known to them, and will continue to make You known in order that the love You have for Me may be in them and that I Myself may be in them* (John 17:24-26).

His life reflected love and He revered and esteemed His Father. Understanding that He must be the unconditional example of love, He willing submitted to that sacrifice. He did not spread out His hands on the cross in vain. He resisted the temptation to come down from the cross at any point. He knew our eternal salvation and the will of His Father depended on His enduring to the end. The agony of the crucifixion and the searing pain raging through His body only served to prove His obedience to the Father. The intense love and grace offered at that time in history cannot be fathomed or understood. External suffering tore His body apart, while at the same time, agonizing torments of hell raged in His spirit. And the reason – love for us and reverence for His Father.

The proof of that rests in words spoken by Him earlier in His ministry: *For I have come down from heaven, not do My will but to do the will of Him who sent Me. And this is the will of Him who sent Me, that I shall lose none of all that He has given Me, but raise them up at the last day. For My Father's will is that everyone who looks to the Son and believes in Him shall have eternal life, and I will raise him up at the last day* (John 6:38-40).

Not only did Jesus Christ desire to fulfill the Father's will and to show a lavish respect and awe for His Father, He planned to provide our spirits with that same ability and desire. As the outpouring of His power flows into our hearts through the Holy Spirit, He enables us to view the Father's amazing love through His example. What amazing grace! What glorious splendor is revealed! Acknowledge an awesome God whose love is beyond comprehension.

Jesus, our Lover, our Bridegroom, cradles our hearts in His hands. Aware of our inability to continually revere and submit to His love and power, He rocks us gently in our circumstances and waits for our cry for help. At even the smallest whimper, He responds and waits and waits and waits. And at just the right moment, He answers the cries and rejoices when we reverently look to Him and extol Him as Lord and Savior. A rejoicing spirit bubbles within when He hears His loved ones say, *I will exalt You, my God the King. I will praise Your name for ever and ever. Every day I will praise You and extol Your name for ever and ever. Great is the Lord and most worthy of praise; His greatness no one can fathom* (Psalm 145:1-3). The surrendered heart sees the Bridegroom for who He is and not for what He can do.

An Influence To Your Husband

The quiet reverence of his wife remained as a focal point for days. Although he knew he appeared stubborn and anxious, she remained calm and ap-

peared to be at rest in something – or someone. He couldn't put his finger on it but he knew it was special. While in his heart he ached for what she had, his stubborn will resisted the thought that perhaps it could be this God she silently, quietly and reverently acknowledged. He saw her meditations, her eyes often closed as if listening for something. Trying to figure out how she could love this God, when so many devastating things happened to her, was far beyond his human comprehension.

It was that spirit that drew him to her in the first place. Assuming she would take anything he had to shell out, he believed that he could get his way and manipulate her into doing his wishes. Yet while submitting to his tantrums did occur, she still spoke up for her standards, her beliefs and her feelings on the issues at hand. He sensed a unique relationship to her God and he couldn't deny the power of it. Yet jealousy reigned for he knew her love for the Lord far surpassed her love for him. He also craved what she had, but didn't want to give in – to admit weakness or defeat.

Many wives today surrender in submission to the Lord as the first step in their marriage relationships. While submission does not mean willingly volunteering to be a battering ram or a crippling enabler to their husbands, it does allow the wife to view everything through the eyes of her true Bridegroom. Submitting to Christ's will and way for her must be primary and only prayer and constant communication with Him can reveal that will. For those with unbelieving husbands, that reverent submission to Jesus Christ creates a sense of peace and joy that only a foolish spouse could deny. Hopefully when seeing the power of Christ in her life and her reverent and faithful witness, his desire will be drawn to the same cross and resurrection in his own life.

Yet for the wife it can be most difficult. Determining whether the relationship's expectations are in line with God's will, because of the dangers it can impose, is difficult and often requires hours of prayer and fasting. Yet when the choice is made, God's peace and abundant joy will result.

Peter tells us in chapter 3, *Wives, in the same way be submissive to your husbands so that, if any of them do not believe the word, they may be won over without words by the behavior of their wives, when they see the purity and reverence of your lives...For this is the way the holy women of the past who put their hope in God used to make themselves beautiful* (Verses 1,2,5).

Please note that the holy women of the past put their hope in God, not in their husbands. Christ, the Bridegroom, must be privileged to be first in our lives. In that submission to a loving, tender, compassionate Husband, we view our earthly relationships through Him. In our reverence for Him in surrender, we discover discernment for our daily lives, one day at a time. It is His wisdom and guidance we follow and to which we willingly yield, one episode at a time, one day at a time. In all our circumstances, we trust His guidance in understanding submission and, when necessary, quietly yield to our husband.

But remember that today, the influence of drugs and alcohol in a marriage build a dangerous atmosphere, unhealthy and unsafe for yourself and your children. Earnestly seek Him and pray for His wisdom. Submission doesn't mean being foolish! It means surrendering first to your true Husband, Jesus Christ, and trusting Him to guide you safely through the ministry and work He has for you to do.

Our Greatest Homage Paid

Offer Him your best. Offer Him a sacrifice of praise. *Through Jesus, therefore, let us continually offer to God a sacrifice of praise – the fruit of lips that confess His name* (Hebrews 13:15).

In the midst of heartache and grief, in the center of turmoil and change, in the heart of one filled with joy or loneliness, offer Him your sacrifice of praise. But you cry, "I can't do it!" And I say to you, "You're right!"

Without Jesus Christ, your true Bridegroom, embracing you and holding your hand, you can't do it. You need Him in ways unimaginable. You humanly struggle to discover what in life has value and worth – certainly void of anything to praise God for. Yet when Jesus Christ enters your life at its very core, changes take place that only He can create. You become new. While the drudgeries of each day appear unending, the pain we encounter frightens our very souls, and the happiness we experience appears temporary, He remains forever. In Him and by Him, we can do everything through Him who gives us strength (Philippians 4:13).

He provides the ability to praise in the midst of the valley of the shadow of death. He enables us to look heavenward and see a loving, protecting Father whose pangs of love for us knows no limits. Then looking through His eyes, we fall on our knees in awe, in reverent submission, in praise for an Almighty God who always has our best interest at heart. We joyfully *sing to Him, sing praise to Him; tell of all His wonderful acts. Glory in His holy name; let the hearts of those who seek the Lord rejoice* (Psalm 105:2-3). Amen and Amen.

Chapter 8

GENTLENESS

Reaching down to touch the flower, she noticed an explosion of sweet-smelling perfume. Hoping to benefit from the beautiful fragrance, she cautiously caressed its velvety petals. Gazing at the intricacy of each petal, the brilliant color, and the fragrance emitted by its very existence, she marveled at the loving tenderness displayed in creating this small sample of God's goodness. Soothed in her spirit, she praised God for the gentle reminder that His goodness rested only a touch away.

Nature envelops us with the wonders of God's creation. The delicate weaving of a snowflake, the rugged but glorious mountain peaks, an indescribable sunset, the tiny, wrinkled hand of a newborn child – all reminders of a God whose love far exceeds our human comprehension.

Bathed in His love, He presents many wonders in our lives. Yet all too often we fail to see the forest for the trees. Focused on the here and now, we see the massive expanse of obstacles standing before us and miss the beauty of the small things revealed on the path or the glory of the larger picture.

Never desiring to rush us through the growth process toward surrender and submission, our Bridegroom gently and tenderly sits close by. Aching for our spirits to trust Him for the overall picture, He desires to remove our dismay and confusion. But we ask, "Which tree do we climb first? There are so many. Do we hide behind the first tree in fear or do we step beyond the tree and move closer to the One who reaches out for us? Lord, there are so many trees – so many obstacles. My job, my children, my husband, my church obligations, all the sports, the busyness, and my feelings of inadequacies– all consume my day. It's hard to climb through the pucker brush and scale the tree and even more difficult to ignore them." Yet He remains patient, assuring us that He is gentle and humble in heart and will continue to wait (Matthew 11:29).

What is this constant ache that lies embedded in our hearts? Rest! Not just physical rest, but rest for our souls. A time of quiet, peace within, a place to hide – that's what we need, Lord. Where can it be found? You say we can find it in You, but how do we get it? Like the precious flower that emitted the beautiful fragrance, we desire to be the perfume of life and love to others. But our lives need first to swallow and absorb all that busyness. Help, Lord! Help!

As we submerge our thoughts with activity, we realize that our cluttered, exploding minds cannot hold much more. "Yet You, dear Jesus, tenderly, gently continue to reach out to us. Your heart aches for our fellowship. 'I have the answer,' You cry. 'Unless you take time first for Me – sometime, somewhere – in your busy schedule, your heart will remain hungering and thirsting for more. You cannot do it without Me. Sit now in a quiet place, close your eyes and ask for My Spirit.'" He awaits your call. He yearns to help you – but will not force Himself upon you. "Now take my Word, that precious book sitting on the dusty shelf, and open it. Discover Me in the Gospels, the Psalms, in Ephesians, in Philippians. They all speak of My gentle love for you. Then, even if you don't 'feel' a change, believe My Spirit is creating a new creature within you. It will be gradual – for I am gentle and humble in heart. I don't push too hard, but know My Spirit can and will create a new person within you. Trust Me. Seek Me. Just do what I ask you to do today – to love Me and to serve Me with all your heart and all your soul. I will take care of the rest."

A Gentle Whisper

In a crowded room, his voice could not be heard. Although she could see his lips move, the thundering noises around smothered the sweet words that flowed from his mouth. How could he make himself heard? What would it take to get her to move closer – to be within a distance of hearing all he wanted to share? Reaching out to her, he motioned to her. But her fear of crossing the sea of people stifled her ability to take even one step in his direction. Yet those eyes – those gentle eyes – kept beckoning her. She knew he wanted her closer. Every fiber of her being ached to be near him. But could she ever step beyond the noise and the chatter to enter the safe abode of his voice? As they stood there – his arms outstretched – he could only wait and pray that eventually she would discover the move toward him to be worth the effort.

In our noisy, crowded lives, our precious Jesus stands with arms outstretched. Crying out to us with a gentleness and tenderness found only in Him, He tries to speak above the thundering noises. As our eyes view Him through His Word, we wonder why we can't get closer. We ache to be near Him but remain fearful when viewing the sea of obstacles – whether real or imaginary – that stand before us. What will it take to move us closer to that voice? How can we really hear above the drone of damaged feelings, fears and frustrations that create images of exploding and impossible walls between us?

Yet He continues to reach out to us. We hear Him cry, "Not only do I want to deal gently and tenderly with you, but I desire to give you those same qualities. As you pass through the sea of muddled faces of despair, loneliness and confusion, each step will bring you closer to the power and might of what I long to give you. Trust Me enough to believe that My Spirit can provide all you need. Your mistakes, your fears, your inadequacies are removed only in Me and I have given you My Spirit to release and free you from those. For that I died. For that, My blood was shed.

"My Father promises to give you all that I have gained for you. As long as you cling to Me, the Vine, and draw closer to My voice, You will experience freedom far beyond your human comprehension, but you must take the steps toward Me. You must keep your eyes on Me and listen for My voice. In time, My voice will drown out the explosive noises of the old man that tells you I am a harsh, unkind Savior. I am gentle and humble in heart. My Father's only desire is to bring you closer to Me for He knows that I intercede on your behalf as a gentle, tender Bridegroom. My plans rest in eternity. My heart for you rests in the cross. I love you and will always be as tender with you as possible. Believe in Me. Trust in Me."

Would We Listen

If we knew our spouses did everything for our best interest, would we willingly submit? If we understood that everything he said, accomplished, and desired for us far outweighed his own personal interests, would it affect our acceptance of him and his love? If all his decisions were based on unconditional love, would we willingly and lovingly respond? If his motives revealed a tender, gentle heart, would we respond in kind?

I cannot help but believe I would personally jump at the chance to listen to such a husband. I would willingly surrender my all to him as I accepted the fact that not one thing would and could be done outside of his love. What an amazing love that would be!

Yet we have a Husband like that. Resting in His unconditional love, Christ totally desires to draw us into His presence and awards us the blessings of His kingdom. Offering His own life on our behalf, He assures us of continual forgiveness and constant guidance – always for our highest good. He gathers up everything in our lives – good and bad, secure and insecure, joyful and grief-smitten – and holds them securely in His tender arms. Promising to hold us close, He draws us into His love. As that love spills into our hearts and His grace and power emerges, His tender, gentle heart becomes ours as well.

Smothered In Thankfulness

She generously slapped the peanut butter and jelly on her sandwich. Piling the second slice of bread on top, she giggled at the thought of enjoying her favorite meal. After all, the more peanut butter and jelly, the more she en-

joyed it. But as she began to chomp her teeth into that sandwich, with all the goodies inside oozing down the sides, her mind recalled days when there was no bread, no peanut butter and no jelly. In fact, food became difficult to find and her belly often became bloated from hunger. The devastation of war held her family in its ravages as warring tribes refused to allow food to pass into the marketplaces. Hours passed into days and days into hours without the nourishing food needed to keep her and her family alive. While trying to live on beetles, grubs and rats, she herself survived but others in her family could not. Now with the luscious sandwich in hand, she chewed, relished and savored every morsel, praising God for the opportunity to again have food on her table and a stomach free of pangs and bloating.

Knowing that a loving God enabled her to survive, she determined to share His goodness with others. While she did not understand why the others had to die, she only knew she must live for Him. He provided the determination to live and gave her the will to trust. Now she must share the grace of His love with others. Just as that peanut butter and jelly oozed down her hand onto the plate, so she believed the tender grace shown to her in the midst of war must ooze into the lives of others. Their plates were empty – not of food but of His goodness. Their hopes dashed into despair, she needed to give that hope to others. And that she did!

How many of us, with full plates and even fuller bellies, could look at the tragedies in our lives as acts of kindness? How many of us with garages overflowing and attics stuffed, care about the revelation of His goodness to others? Are we so used to steaks that peanut butter and jelly strikes our pallets like lead – tasteless and beneath our status? What has happened to us? Why is it that only those who hunger the most, truly see past the surface to discover the spiritual grace and goodness found only in Christ?

Perhaps it is because that when all else is gone, Christ embodies all we need. When the stripping of the veneer of our lives cannot be eluded, we see our greatest need – His tenderness, His peace, and His power. We cry out, "Christ is enough. He is what I truly need!"

As we surrender to Him, Christ is willing to gently strip away the things in our lives that hold us back. In the process, He promises to recreate in us new, redeemed, enlivened creatures. Seeing His love, forgiveness and gentleness, we rejoice in the small pleasures given, the privileges bestowed, and the power revealed. Then because we cannot keep the inner blessings quiet, we pray for opportunities to share that love with others. The gentleness of our Bridegroom flows through us into the lives of others and explodes into a flurry of constant, persistent sharing. Holding closely to our Creator, we dance with joy, even over peanut butter and jelly – for it is the simple things that make us happy. We have truly discovered that, after all, Christ is enough. Christ is all we need.

Chapter 9

A QUIET SPIRIT

Questions, accusations, and lies spilled out of the mouths of His accusers, yet He stood before them silent. If He spoke at all, He spoke only truth – not justification. His place in the kingdom needed no justification. The lies mattered not. He wasn't surprised for He knew they would come. Yet He remained silent.

Three different officials questioned him. He remained silent. Mockery preceded beatings, cruel hands slapped Him and still, more lies. But He remained silent. Why? Why didn't He speak up? How could He remain quiet during such a time as this?

Did He not know where it was leading? Didn't He possess foreknowledge of the leather whip that would gouge deeply into His flesh; the crown of thorns to be forced upon His head; the weight of the wooden cross soon to be thrown across His shoulders? What about the dividing of His clothing; the nails driven into His wrists; the awful crucifixion – the suffocating feeling, the thirst, the searing pain throughout His body? If He knew, why would He remain silent?

Love moved Him forward. An all-encompassing love for His Father weighed heavily on Him as He centered His life on doing the Father's will. An unconditional love for us kept Him quiet in the midst of injustice and torment. Although a legion of angels could have rescued Him, He chose the scourging, the torment, the torture – all for love. That is what kept Him quiet.

Without complaint and with a heart of courage difficult for most to imagine, love moved Him forward. Not only the physical torment proved intolerable, but the hell of spiritual separation from His Father created an agony beyond description. The demons scoffed and sneered as they viewed Him on the cross. They assumed they had won.

But, oh, the victory of obedience – the joy that He embraced and experienced at the end result – the salvation of our souls! He faced shame, pain and disgrace for love. Through obedience, He not only revealed love but reflected it. And He did it with a quiet spirit.

Come To A Quiet Place

Johnny entered the dark, quiet place. He desired refreshment for his weary soul. He expected a peaceful covering but encountered none. Anxiety overwhelmed him. Despair loomed before him as a sharp blade cutting into his heart, deeper and deeper. Why wouldn't the Lord listen? What was he doing wrong?

Unable to stand it any longer, he decided to take his own life. If God wouldn't heed his call, what hope was there? Life held so many dark places and relief could not be found. Even the quiet places appeared as a lashing whip punishing him for all the wrong he had done. Unworthiness, lack of acceptance and despair covered his back and the burden weighed his spirit down beyond comprehension.

Without warning, a sliver of light flooded the quiet, dark room. Unsure from where it came, he looked around for the source, but found none. Falling on his knees, he tried to catch the light in his hands. As the ray of light settled on his fingers, he allowed it to move up his arms. Suddenly he realized that the light rested and stopped on his heart – his cold, despairing heart.

Touching his heart with the tenderness of a mother, he closed his eyes and cried for the first time in weeks. "Oh, God, I can't! I just can't do it anymore. I went to the quiet place, but it didn't help. I thought just being there would be enough. But it wasn't. I can't handle even one minute without You. I am unable to understand what is happening and why, but I know I need You. Without You there is only darkness. Give me the quietness and rest I crave. I hunger for it. Tell me where to go and I will search for it to the end of my days. Guide me, Jesus, guide me!"

On the hard, cold ground, he discovered a rest and quietness never known before. Lying still and motionless for many minutes, he experienced the Savior's love and peace beyond comprehension. What he tried to do for days, the God of mercy accomplished in an instant. Admitting his helplessness, he turned to the Source of the quietness. Rather than a planned place of his chosen quietness, he found the quiet deep within – provided by God who waited for his call and his brokenness of spirit.

Letting the ray of light rest in his hand, he rejoiced in the newly-found love. He realized that the quiet place isn't a location – it's the deep abiding presence of His Savior, Jesus Christ.

As it was with Johnny, so it is with us. In our moments of despair, in the midst of difficult circumstances, hungering for more than life has to offer, Christ enters our very beings to strengthen and support. He is the quiet place. He is the source of our peaceful moments. Holding out His loving hands, He beckons us with the words, *I am with you. I am mighty to save. I will take great delight in you. I will quiet you with My love. I will rejoice over you with singing* (Zephaniah 3:17).

Calmness When Confronted

So how do I know when to stay quiet? How can I maintain the posture Christ Jesus held at His trial? He remained quiet in the midst of accusations and lies. As a sheep before its shearers, He did not open His mouth in retaliation or defense. He spoke only when the truth needed to be heard and He knew the difference (Isaiah 53:7).

But I always want to defend myself. When people say unkind things about me, I must prove them wrong. Angered and desiring to respond with "my side of the story," I speak up and speak loudly.

I know meekness does not mean timidity or weakness, yet that's the way I feel when I don't defend myself. I want to shout my innocence from the rooftops. I want to prove that their accusations hold no ground and possess no truth.

As an example, He remained quiet before His accusers. When will I learn how to follow His lead? Is there a magic prayer or an exciting quote I can repeat when the going gets sticky? Or maybe surrender and humble prayer are the answer.

The true answer is: His Spirit does all the work. His Spirit makes all the changes – simply for the asking. We may not feel it or even notice the change, but it will happen. Why? Because He promised it will. It is a gift from the Bridegroom.

"Jesus, my Bridegroom, I need to learn from You. Truth dwells within You for, in fact, You are Truth. With truth, there is no need for retaliation or justification. Knowing and accepting You as Truth, I can face the falsehood and lies. As my Bridegroom, I acknowledge that, when called upon, Your Truth will flow into me. Give me the strength to call on You and to acknowledge you as Truth. Remove my pride, my selfishness, and my need to avenge or retaliate. Only in You can I speak the truth in love, void of the big word 'I'. The power of the Spirit is Yours to give and You willingly provide that power, simply for the asking. I am asking for that now, dear Jesus. In Your name, I pray. Amen."

Father, How Could You Remain Quiet?

"Father, You saw Him bleeding. You saw the brutality to which Jesus succumbed. You witnessed the beating, the bloodied back, the deep, gaping cuts in His scalp from the crown of thorns. You must have wept. No! You must have agonized. Like a searing knife cutting into a chunk of meat, Your heart must have felt every blade of the whip, every scream of pain, and every nail pounded into His flesh. He was not only Your Son – Your only Son – but He shared a oneness with You from eternity.

"You witnessed the creation together. Your love shared in the boldness of the prophets, the apostles, and other holy ones filled with Your Spirit. Your love guided the children across the Red Sea and remained close to the chosen people in a cloud and pillar of fire.

Lives, hearts and love connected You in a manner no man can comprehend.

"But at His crucifixion, You watched and remained quiet. Grieving over Your Son's torment, You experienced the torment in greater measure. You could not bend down and save Him. Love must prevail. Love must endure. Love must save the others. Oh, the depth of Your love – to sacrifice the One You loved so much for the sake of all the others.

"You smelled the stench of sin. It covered and consumed Your Son – Your sinless Son. He must suffer for those sins – those sins of all time and all peoples. You must turn Your back – not because You didn't love, but because You did. But only for a blink of time in realm of eternity."

As the angels awaited the word from the Father, they stood ready to save His Son. How quiet they were – determinedly quiet. Gut-wrenching silence filled the heavens as they too witnessed the horrors of the One they loved so deeply. Why doesn't the Father stop all this hideousness? When the cry entered the heavens, *My God, my God, why have You forsaken Me?* they shuddered (Matthew 27:46). But turning to the Father, they witnessed His face turned away from the sin – the hideous sin. The stench even to them appeared unbearable.

Satan rejoiced. His army of demons danced with glee. They had won! Or did they?

No Greater Love Than This

The agony of the cross ended with the words, *Father, into Your hands I commit my spirit* (Luke 23:46).

The Father's agony ceased. Now He rejoiced. His Son's completed work. The blood sacrifice of the Lamb, in the greater and more perfect tabernacle in heaven, released a flood of pure, undefiled incense. The aroma of salvation, of eternal forgiveness and of love filled the heavenlies. The angels bathed in its fragrance. They now understood. They knew the sacrifice of the Father and the Son to be worth the price. The eternal surprise – an eternity with a host of those arrayed in white, washed in the blood of the Lamb. The Son paid the price – once for all.

Satan still didn't understand. Why was heaven rejoicing when Christ still lay in the tomb? He died and could no longer challenge Satan's diligent work of destroying others. Satan hated these people and wanted their destruction. He desired a lifetime of hell for them. After all, he wanted as many with him in hell as possible. Why should he and his armies endure God's wrath alone?

But he forgot the truth – truth spoken many times by Jesus Himself. The grave would not hold Him. Satan would be overcome. Death would not hold victory. The Suffering Christ became the Risen Christ. Death and the grave held Him not.

Satan lost.

The ultimate truth – we have also victory – not because of anything we have done, but because of Truth. Christ and the Father held that truth before them every inch of the way. Now, *let us fix our eyes on Jesus, the author and perfector of our faith, who for the joy set before Him, Christ endured the cross, scorning its shame and sat down at the right hand of the throne of God. Consider him who endured such opposition from sinful men, so that you will not grow weary and lose heart* (Hebrews 12:2-3).

What occurs when we inherit our Bridegroom's quiet spirit? Our boldness increases. Our faith abounds. Our love multiplies. A willingness to seek the wisdom and guidance of a sacrificial Lamb in the midst of accusations, of lies and of falsehoods opens multitudes of doors for an appropriate quiet spirit. Unite with the Lamb! In Him and in Him alone rests the power of His quiet Spirit.

Chapter 10

FREEDOM FROM FEAR

He crouched in the corner, frightened by every noise that seemingly exploded in his ears. No one consoled him. No one assured him that the noises he heard were harmless play. He sensed despair and utter rejection, which only heightened the intensity of what already gripped his heart. How and when would it all end? When would the magical trumpet blow and release him from the fear that absorbed all his thoughts and actions?

She lay in bed consumed with fear, heightened by stiff muscles, profuse sweating and intense headaches. Closing her eyes, she had to believe that someone would come and melt away the fear. She hated the enhanced physical and emotional stress it created in her life, but knew little about ridding herself of the dreadful presence that dominated her being – the presence of fear. It stabbed her during the day and consumed her at night. How and when would it all end? When would God send His magical trumpet to blow it away?

These two different scenarios display the horrors and extreme outcomes of fear. Each encounters fear and reacts differently, but both must come to terms with it or remain crippled forever.

In the first case, the fears of the little boy remained for a lifetime. His memory tried to erase the noises of abuse, even the small ones, but they spiraled him into his corner of reality, fearful of everything and everyone. Secluded and alone, he never found that one individual who could rescue him and pull him from his pit of despair.

However, the young lady in the second situation grew dramatically from her existence of fear. Resolved to discover an answer and to smother herself in God's love, she gradually embraced His goodness in her life. One day at a time, she recognized that He could and would overcome. Recovery was not instantaneous, for restoration took months. But in the process, she learned that her Bridegroom, the precious Jesus Christ, remained true and constant. Her Perfect Love cast out fear and replaced it with a deep love – for Him and for others.

Though fear did resurface, she cast it out by the constant mention of His name. No longer consumed by fear, she cherished the Savior's presence in her life. In trust she continued to turn to Him and rest in Him. It is that trust, that turning toward His comely face, which chased the fear away. Alone, she could not accomplish the dismissal of the ravages of it. But, in Him, it was rubbed out. In its place, she found peace and comfort. His amazing love took the place of the crippling fear.

A Rocking Boat

Picture if you will, a rocking boat in the midst of a tempest. Waves and swells from the churning water threaten the lives of those on board. Filled with terror, the oarsmen row with strenuous determination, but to no avail. The water gushes into the boat from the raging waters of the lake and the drenching rain from heaven. Yet, there He is. Sound asleep. Can you believe it? Instead of crouching in fear, or helping the oarsmen in their struggle, He sleeps – like a baby.

Finally in desperation, they cry out, "Lord, don't you care that we'll die? This boat will soon go down and you just keep sleeping. You're our Lord and Master. Do something!"

Aroused from His sleep, Jesus looks at the awestruck men, and asks, "O men of little faith! Why are you so afraid?"

Then He calmly reaches forth His hand and says, "Peace, be still."

Amazingly, it was not the oarsmen who listened first. The very winds and waves, that created havoc in their lives listened first. With eyes that must have popped out of their heads and minds totally stunned by His control over nature, they declared, *What kind of man is this? Even the winds and waves obey Him!* (Matthew 8:23-26).

Staggering, isn't it? Yet confusing as well. How could one not be frightened in a storm that crashes violently into our lives? Is not fear a natural human emotion? Didn't Jesus, Himself, experience extreme anguish and sorrow in the garden of Gethsemane?

While I admit I don't have all the answers, I have experienced overwhelming fear. I know it can create detrimental physical, emotional and spiritual torture. And Satan's greatest desire is to deeply embed it into our souls, destroying our hopes and dreams. With each crippling blow of fear, he desires that we cower in a corner, rather than step forward in faith. Even as the trumpet of Christ's mercy and love blows into our lives, Satan, as a roaring lion, convinces us that the fear is more powerful and more ingrained. "There is no hope," Satan shouts. "Your Bridegroom cannot help. You are on your own and you will lose."

How false! What a lie! As Christ raised His hand and controlled the power of the surging waves, the angry wind and the pounding rain, so He can and does calm our battles with fear. But it takes courage – His courage – to raise a fist to Satan and say "Enough is enough! I claim victory in Jesus Christ."

While the winds and the waves obeyed instantly, Christ doesn't always instantly remove the storms in our lives. Rather than calming the storms that rage around us, He calms us in the midst of that storm. He provides a confidence and assurance that He is in control and that, when His mighty eternal purposes are complete, He will restore us and bring an end to the storm.

I am always comforted by the verse in 1 Peter 5:10, *And the God of all grace, who called you to his eternal glory in Christ, after you have suffered a little while, will himself restore you and make you strong, firm and steadfast*. Please note that after the storm, the time of suffering, He *Himself* will restore you. He *Himself* will make you strong. He *Himself* will enable you to be firm and steadfast. The strength does not come from our own being. It comes from Him. He alone provides the freedom from fear and sheds the emotional attachments to it. And it will be accomplished much like the peeling of an onion, one layer at a time and most of the time with the shedding of tears.

Christ's Response To Fear

So how did Christ's fearful reaction to the impending torture of hell differ from the screaming fishermen in the rocking boat? Why did His fear appear more intense, His sorrow deeper and His anguish more excruciating?

I believe with all my heart and soul that Christ, coming into this world of sin, experienced every emotion common to man – fear included. Gripped with the foreknowledge that He would be betrayed, deserted, on trial, tortured, and crucified, He experienced the extreme of fear – so much so that His sweat became as great drops of blood. Yet the intense fear to end all fears was not the knowledge of His suffering and death but that of a total separation from the presence of His Father. The glories of heaven, the all-consuming love, the relationship He shared for an eternity was soon to be severed and He would be alone – totally alone. That fear created the agony of spirit deeper than any man shall know in this lifetime. Only in eternity will the lost understand that agony – and for that the King, Savior and Bridegroom endured it all. How He wishes we would listen! How He craves and desires that we believe His extreme price manifested in His fear – a fear we don't need to experience.

Why was it different with the fishermen? The presence of Christ lay only a few feet away! Did they not believe in His protecting care? Were they so unsure of His divine command over the forces of nature, that they assumed the worst?

Yet daily, hourly and monthly, we find ourselves in those same rocking boats. Storms rage. They flood our beings with fear. But what do we do with them? Do we struggle against the waves or do we rest next to His presence? Do we see only the sleeping Savior or do we believe His presence is more powerful than any wave that splashes into our boat? Wherein is our security? Can we truly see the waves, the storms, the rocking boat as a blessing?

Therein lies the difference. Christ was to be totally and completely separated from the Father's love – no presence of good anywhere. We, however, always have Christ's presence within us. He dwells in our spirits. He rejoices with us in the victories found in Him and grants us the courage to step beyond our fears. Keeping our eyes on Him rather than the waves, we are strengthened by the Holy Spirit. The calm rests within. *Even though I walk through the valley of the shadow of death, I will fear no evil, for you are with me; your rod and your staff, they comfort me* (Psalm 23:4).

Hard To Trust

Plastered against the wall glistened the residue from the day before. The parade of clowns, movie stars, and balloons ran through her mind like a video tape. Everyone enjoyed the event – everyone, that is, except her. She was the star. People applauded. Teenagers screamed. Starry-eyed, adoring fans cried at her presence.

But the wall served as a powerful reminder of what should have been, but only erased the joy she wanted to feel. Closing her eyes, she relived the events of the preceding day. As a young child approached her car, a gun-like object slowly pointed directly at her. Terrified beyond all comprehension, she froze in fear. Yet in the next instant, the impact of the child's display of affection became emblazoned in her memory. First came the explosion. Then, the splatter of glitter and confetti blew at her, nearly forcing her over the back of the car. An expression of the child's adoration splashed into her life as the most horrifying experience encountered.

Immediately after the explosion, hundreds of adoring fans mobbed her. Carnage reigned. The bodyguards used every method of shelter possible, but only brute force could free her from the clinging arms and groping hands. Many just wanted to touch her. Most just wanted a piece of the action, or a piece of her. Their expressions of admiration only compounded the already difficult circumstances.

Now today, looking at the glitter-splattered wall, she wept. The feelings of horror, terror and fear all resurfaced. How could the child have assumed that her mode of admiration and flattery would be understood? Didn't she evaluate the possibility that it could create fear rather than admiration?

"When will it end?" she sobbed. "I worked so hard to become a celebrity, but now wish I could only seclude myself behind a high, fenced wall. I hate the fears and don't know how to resolve them. When will it all end?"

Behind our fenced walls, we seek solitude. We desire to be a recluse. As the mountains of adoring fans scream for our attention, we cry, "When will it all end?" As children cling to our arms and grope for affection with their hands, we fear that we don't have the strength to bear up under their needs and expectations. As husbands, bosses and relatives explode their demands on our time and energies, we huddle and cry for an escape. As we look at the glittered walls of what we thought it would be, we cry in despair and say, "Enough! I've had enough!"

Some women only encounter small fears. Others encounter fears of deep intensity. They ache for a bodyguard to pull them to shelter. Fear sweeps away the joy of service and only expectations are left. The demands, the screams and cries of others swallow us up. "When will it end? When will it all end?" we cry. "It's hardly what I expected. I wanted the attention but now I feel it is more than I can handle. And the fears seem to multiply every day. I want the fears to go away, but just don't know how. Please, someone, show me how!"

I hear of women who leave their husbands and families to seek a "better" life. More and more women experience anxiety and panic attacks. The reliance on drugs and alcohol brings seeming temporary relief, while the undercurrent of emotions, low self-esteem and fear is suffocated and ignored. As the conditions worsen, so do the fears. Yet the fears then create a greater need for more drugs, more alcohol, and relief from more panic attacks. "When will it end? When will it all end?"

Oh, our precious Jesus weeps for those caught in its web! As He views the carnage, the fear, the loneliness, He offers Himself as the answer. Yet all too many believe He cannot accomplish the satisfaction and rest behind the walls they seek. Determined to solve the issues of fear and despair alone, they continue to wait for their dream bodyguard to come to their rescue. They continue the drugs, the alcohol, the dependence on self and others. Or worse, they hide behind those make-believe walls, alone and afraid, with no means of penetration. There, they believe, no one can hurt them.

Fear steals His life-giving presence from us. It closes the door to the Bridegroom and opens the door to the despair that Satan desires for us. His elation over our fear and despair explodes in our faces, much like the explosion of glitter and confetti. The only difference – he is not our fan. He is our enemy. And his greatest desire is to keep us from the joy, the peace and the freedom that your biggest Fan yearns to pass on to you. Jesus Christ knows fear. He experienced the ultimate fear – the absence of God the Father and His eternal, unconditional love. Don't be stripped of this precious gift from the Bridegroom, who wants to flood you with His love. Turn to Him in your fears – both great and small – and give Him the permission to free you from Satan's hold through praise – constant praise. Let the chains fall. Let freedom reign.

Fear not, for I have redeemed you; I have summoned you by name; you are mine. When you pass through the waters, I will be with you; and when you pass through the rivers, they will not sweep over you. When you walk through the fire, you will not be burned; the flames will not set you ablaze. For I am the Lord, your God, the Holy One of Israel, your Savior (Isaiah 43:1b-3a).

Chapter 11

A TRUSTING HEART

A power surge occurred. In that instant, numerous changes manifested themselves. Most lights dimmed. Others lit up brightly. Several clocks needed to be reset. The answering machine announced its desire to be reprogrammed. While only minor irritations, they created more energy inside me than could be calculated in the house. The corrections became as frustrating to me as a child scratching his fingernails down a chalkboard. The screeching halt to my activities neither pleased me nor enabled me to continue my day without making the minor adjustments.

Not everyone is bothered by the insignificant exasperation of an electrical surge, yet the minor disruptions of this life compound and magnify our already wearied spirits and bodies. Coming home from work on a crowded highway creates anger and impatience. Crying babies, dirty diapers, expectations of husbands, and strong-willed children all scratch down our spine like a child's fingers on a chalkboard. In our busy, harried lives these irritations manifest themselves as a power surge – with small, sudden breakdowns in patience, in gentleness and in compassion. Personalities that often may appear loving and kind explode in a frenzy of anger, tears and depression.

Not having the internal strength to cry out to God and say, "Help," we struggle on our own, hoping it will get better tomorrow, sure that our own strength will hold up and the messes from today will resolve themselves. Unfortunately, all too often, they carry over into our lives another day and the power surge begins again and the little breakdowns add to the irritations from the day before.

Within a short time span, we wonder where all the power went and throw up our hands in despair. It never occurred to us that our busy schedules fail to include a special, meaningful time with the

Bridegroom. The big, enormous rooms of our hearts, filled with busy schedules, lack of desire and dependence on self, leave little space for the One who desires to cushion the blows and soften the harshness.

In the meantime, the Lord waits in the corners, the hallways, and the closets of our hearts and minds. His presence dances behind the scenes hoping to create a generous, giving heart. Exploding with many power surges, the living Christ sits and continues to call us to Him. The difference – His power surges will energize, not create additional irritations to our already busy lives. He won't force Himself upon us but patiently waits for attention to be turned His way.

How far do we have to go before we realize the power void we experience without Him in our lives? What extreme in daily power surges do we need before we surrender to the power surges of His Holy Spirit? Do we wait for breakdown city before we fall on bended knee to succumb to all the intense love and grace He desires to spill into our lives? What will it take?

A desperate father once cried, "Lord, *I do believe; help me overcome my unbelief!*" (Mark 9:24). Herein lies the solution. The answer to a lack of trust centers in the fact that we, on our own, must relay trust, as minute as it may be – then ask Him to supply the additional trust. He craves to enter the enormous rooms of our hearts and fill them to overflowing, but we must open the doors. And that, through the Holy Spirit, takes an admission of our own weakness and the cry for help. As the Spirit knocks, we must turn the doorknob and open the door for His entry. Oh, how He craves that entry! What an abundance of goodness floods into our lives as we grant Him permission to take over **every** room in our heart – not just the corners, the hallways and the closets! He wants to fill you with His fullness. Are you ready? Are you willing?

How Sweet It Is!

One of the tastiest dishes I have ever eaten is sweet, buttery whipped cream served over a heaping bowl of strawberries. Growing up with grandparents who were farmers, I remember being a recipient of their luscious produce. Homemade fresh butter, heavy whipped cream on pies, homemade bread, freshly butchered meat, garden vegetables – either fresh from the garden or home-canned – graced our tables. In addition we participated in the graciousness of Grandma's hospitality, which she generously doled out to us. Thanksgiving meals, especially, remain intact in my mind as events worth storing for an eternity.

Jesus Christ can't wait to fill our tables with His abundant goodness, full to overflowing with all the spiritual food we can imagine or desire. There is no end. His wisdom, His understanding and His insight wait for us in heaping bowls, on luscious tables and surrounded with amazing tasty goodness, yet all too often we reject them for the things of this life. His inviting Thanksgiving feast remains for an eternity, while our meals of self-desire prove temporary and must be filled again tomorrow. We need to remember: *Therefore we do not lose heart. Though outwardly we are wasting away, yet inwardly we are being renewed day by day. For our light and momentary troubles are achieving for us an eternal glory that far outweighs them all. So we fix our eyes not on what is seen, but on what is unseen. For what is seen is temporary, but what is unseen is eternal* (2 Corinthians 4:17-18).

While shaking over our shattered world, we must turn to Him in trust. Storing up and building anger, frustration and questions about life and about God, we must continue to trust. When life makes no sense and we want to throw up our hands in despair, we cry to Him for additional trust. When our child becomes violently ill, we must trust and, when we can't, rely on Him to fill us with His power to trust. When a parent or spouse or another loved one dies, we turn to Him in faith. Even when it doesn't make sense and our minds shout, "Give up on God," we must clinch our fists and scream, "No, I will not give up on God."

Otherwise, you see, Satan wins. He overtakes our mind with hatred, bitterness, revenge, and an unforgiving heart. He tempts us to scrap all of God's goodness. This will stagnate our spirit and create heartache and anger difficult to overcome. Release your questioning heart into His open arms. Accept the penitential sacrifice on the cross and believe that He understands and forgives. A trusting heart will be rewarded. He anxiously waits to open doors for us to receive His insight and understanding beyond human comprehension.

Straight Paths

Trust in the Lord with all your heart and lean not on your own understanding; in all your ways acknowledge Him, and He will make your paths straight (Proverbs 3:5-6).

I once used a phrase, "When in doubt, leave it out!" If I was doing research on a particular subject or needed knowledge about a particular topic, rather than go to someone who could help me discover the missing information, I would leave it out of the presentation. Avoiding it altogether was easier that seeking a source of wisdom on the subject.

Yet daily that is what many of us do in our lives. We desire to know the answers to the pounding questions and the difficult decisions but refuse to look for guidance. Deciding to prove our own capabilities, we ask ourselves, "Who could know better than I? And if I don't know, I will just leave it out. It's easier than having to seek answers to this life, with all its messes. Wading through the muck and mire is easier than seeking the wisdom and guidance of the Lord. Just make it easy. Right?"

Wrong! Life's challenges fill our lives for the purpose of growth. The difficult times create perseverance and courage. The impossibilities become possible, not because we possess the wisdom but because we know the Source of wisdom. Alone, we may never adequately discover our full potential. But Christ, our wise Bridegroom, cuts a path of honor and goodness before us, pleading with us to follow Him. But that requires trust and a turning toward His goodness. Learn to grasp all that He has to give – it will last a lifetime.

In our daily walk with God, we cannot expect Him to pour out

His abundant pleasures as we sit apathetically in His presence. With no devotional time, no pleasure in His Word, no relational, quality time in prayer and no trust in His eternal purposes of our lives, we squander the hours of each day without Him, content to avoid and belittle His grace. With each stinging slap of our hands not folded in prayer, with each grumbling word that slides over our mouths, and with each verbal word of discontentment as to His supply, we push Him deeper away from our inner being and self takes over. Yet until His presence takes rest in our hearts, our soul will stumble, slide and slip through life without Him – because we think it's easier to leave Him out than to seek Him out.

Desiring to guide you on level ground, He sometimes pulls you over mountains and through valleys, in hopes that somewhere, somehow you will realize the void that can only be filled with Him. He desires to give you a steadfast, trusting heart – but for us, that takes exercise. As our muscles atrophy without any sign of exercise, so our faith atrophies without daily exercise in His presence. The steps are up to us – the path is up to Him.

Hezekiah's Trust

Hezekiah trusted in the Lord, the God of Israel. There was no one like him among all the kings of Judah, either before him or after him. He held fast to the Lord and did not cease to follow Him; he kept the commands that Lord had given Moses. And the Lord was with him; he was successful in whatever he undertook (2 Kings 18:5-7a).

Scripture tells us that *the Lord's unfailing love surrounds the man who trusts in him* (Psalm 32:10b). Hezekiah exemplified that trust. When belittled, mocked and threatened by the king of Assyria, he tore his clothes, put on sackcloth and went into the temple of the Lord. He ordered his palace administrator, the secretary and all the leading priests to do the same. He then sent them to Isaiah, the prophet, for comfort and wisdom.

The words of Isaiah, shining words of God's wisdom, lightened the heart and soul of Hezekiah. *Tell your master, 'This is what the*

Lord says: Do not be afraid of what you have heard – those words with which the underlings of the king of Assyria have blasphemed Me. Listen! I am going to put such a spirit in him that when he hears a certain report, he will return to his own country, and there I will have him cut down with the sword. And so it happened (2 Kings 19:6-7).

Hezekiah trusted God to provide a way of escape. Hezekiah believed that seeking the source of his strength would bring about the salvation of his people. And God rewarded that trust.

Even in his illness, he trusted the Lord to grant him longer days. And God not only answered that prayer but gave him a sign by allowing the sun to go back ten steps – nothing of which ever occurred before or after on earth. His trust received rewards.

And so will yours. Capture His goodness in this life as you reflect a trust in Him no matter how difficult or trying your circumstances. Rejoice in His provision as you observe Him opening doors for your ministry and mission. Overcome the temptations of Satan as you resist his fierce fight to win you over to his designed destruction. Explode with the energy of the Spirit as you say with Isaiah, *Surely this is our God; we trusted in Him, and He saved us. This is the Lord, we trusted in Him; let us rejoice and be glad in His salvation* (Isaiah 25:9).

Trust carries rich rewards. Embrace them daily. Practice them faithfully. Absorb them like a sponge. For *blessed is the man who trusts in the Lord, whose confidence is in Him. He will be like a tree planted by the water that sends out its roots by the stream. It does not fear when heat comes; its leaves are always green. It has no worries in a year of drought and never fails to bear fruit* (Jeremiah 17:7-8).

Chapter 12

UNRELENTING LOVE

He captured their hearts. Adored by men and women alike, few believed the news regarding the atrocities. He satisfied their lonely demands. He confirmed their coveted desires. He gave them what they wanted and more. How could they turn their back on such a man? He provided a government they could believe in for he seemed to rescue them from their present difficulties and provide hope for the future.

Another man, however, spoke of submission. He spoke of a kingdom beyond comprehension. He displayed an unusual love and spoke of forgiving others, even the enemy. Rather than giving them a chicken in every pot, He expected them to give up things. Hardly a man to follow! Hardly a man to rescue them from the government they so hated!

Two different men – one appeared to be a rescuer; the other proved to be a disappointment. One seemingly filled with answers for the physical needs and desires of man; the other asking for surrender, for sacrifice, for persecution. The first man was Hitler; the second man was Jesus Christ.

How can we be so mistaken in life? What drives people to believe that a destructive, violent man such as Hitler could save most but allows them to reject the Savior of their very souls? Is the material more important than the spiritual? Does the here-and-now capture our mind and rationale before that which fills our inner man with good things? What does Jesus Christ have to offer that far outweighs the material blessings an earthly rescuer provides? Peace won't fill a stomach. Joy won't pay the bills. A long-suffering spirit won't satisfy the need for a big home, fancy car and big checking account.

When a seemingly good earthly leader promises all those things, why would we turn to a so-called Savior who only guides us through the tough spots or holds our hand as we walk through the valley of the shadow of death? I want to live for what is visible and will satisfy me today. How can Jesus do that? What does He do for me that no man can?

Sunken in a quagmire of despair, attitudes change. Terminal illness shrouds our spirits with the darkness and we cry for strength beyond ourselves. When stomachs churn and sicknesses invade, the ache for appetite submerges. Oh, how we crave for a day without pain, without a sickened stomach or without the fatigue that wears away at our bodies. Turning to the earthly leader means little. The "chicken in every pot" matters little for we have no hunger – no desire to enjoy that chicken. Our bones dry up within and we crave a rescuer who can enter the inner man with understanding, with patience, with peace. In healthy times and good days, the earthly pride elevates. But in times of drought and of despair, we begin to understand the difference between the two leaders. One brings temporary relief, the other eternal sustenance. One supplies our bodies; the other nourishes our souls. One slaps us on the back, craving self-acknowledgment; the other soothes our agonized spirit, yearning for a permanent relationship and the well-being of the hurting body and soul. Who would you rather trust to restore you and uphold you? Where do you turn when the chips are really down? Which do you now prefer to have filled – the void of greed or the void of the inner, aching spirit?

Driven By Love

Jesus said, *My command is this: Love each other as I have loved you. Greater love has no one than this, that he lay down his life for his friends. You are my friends if you do what I command* (John 15:12-14).

Lay down your life in service. Lay it down in sacrifice. Lay it down in selfless love – thinking of others first. Love your enemies.

Blessed are the meek, gentle, humble. Blessed are the merciful. Blessed are the pure in heart. Blessed are you when you are persecuted because of righteousness. Love My Father. Obey His commands. Be men of courage. Do everything in love. Know the love that surpasses knowledge. May your love overflow for others. Love one another deeply.

A love dedicated to the kingdom of God and to the person of Jesus Christ makes little sense. The demands seem backward and foreign in this land. It requires a lowering of self and an elevating of someone unseen. It displays forgiveness when revenge is desired. It showers blessing on others when we desire the blessings ourselves. It serves without expecting anything in return. It endures, it trusts, it perseveres.

Oh, my precious Bridegroom, aren't You expecting the impossible? Isn't the way of all flesh so much easier than the demands You make upon me? Wouldn't it be easier to follow the other leaders in my life – wealth, prosperity, fame, control, material possessions? You're asking me to give up too much. Why do You expect the opposite of what I desire? Why do You make it so hard?

The Bridegroom answers, "Because what I am asking you to do is not dependent on you. The quest for inner strength, power, joy and love – unrelenting love – does not spill out of you willingly. When you rely on self, it does not happen. Like sucking in your gut to hide an overweight belly, loving others without My Spirit proves hopeless. You cannot desire the best for others, without expecting a return. You will not crave a deep heartfelt interest and concern for those around you, unless My Spirit fills you and covers you with layer upon layer of My strength and power. I supply it – as needed – for each situation. But it must come from Me. When left to your own devices and whims, the wrong words, the nasty implications, the faulty wiring of self will bring forth the wrong leader in your life. You must desire to fill your spirit with My life-giving love. One is temporary, the other eternal. Trust Me to give you the better of the two. Rely on Me to give you an overabundance of an incredible love unknown to you before. It can and will come. I can and will supply it."

We struggle and resist but His love cries out in inexpressible words. His Spirit pleads with us through His Word, His friends, and His gentle reminders – yet we turn a deaf ear. We crave the leader who supplies today's desires, not the One who overflows with spiritual and physical abundance, through His timing and His wisdom. When will we learn? When will we accept the abundant, unrelenting love that covers and protects us through the rough paths, the choppy seas, and the unwelcome waters of our lives? When allowing them to enter our lives, He uses them to draw us to Him. All are messages of love, coupled with His agonizing tears. Pleading and begging for us to turn to Him, to accept His love that flowed on the cross of Calvary, He continues to keep an ever-watchful eye upon us. He can't change us unless we desire a change. He won't interfere with our choices against Him, but agonizes when we do. His unrelenting love knocks – no, pounds – on the door of our hearts and tenderly says, "I love you. Please accept My gift of love. I laid down My life for you. I want to fill you to overflowing with that love. I want you to understand how wide and long and high and deep is My love and to know this love that surpasses knowledge. Every fiber of My body and soul aches to reveal that love. Please open the door. Please listen to My Spirit's pleading."

The More You Give Away, The More You Receive

Now to Him who is able to do immeasurably more than all we ask or imagine, according to His power that is at work within us, to Him be glory in the church and in Christ Jesus throughout all generations, for ever and ever! Amen (Ephesians 3:20-21).

There is a phrase that says, "Love isn't love until it's given away." In the example of a small child, that love is evident. When cuddled, rocked, and soothed, the child succumbs to the loving accolades of the giver of love. Yet the child may not say a thing. Just the quiet surrender to a love given away fills the heart of every parent, grandparent, aunt, uncle, or sibling. The treasure lies not in the return of the love but in the giving of it. The warmth and the serenity impassioned in the calmness of the child is all our hearts needs and requires in return. Trust and security is displayed. Clothed with the contentment of giving away to someone else, we receive back in abundance. That is love.

Everywhere hurting people rebel. Children join gangs to find acceptance. Spouses leave because their desires remain unfulfilled. Selfishness abounds. Yet all too often they desire and crave for acceptance. Perceiving that the receiving of love is what they need, they look for it in all the wrong places.

They don't realize that the cry of their hearts could be soothed in the act of serving others in love. Assisting in nursing homes where many lonely, despairing people simply exist day after day; working with mentally handicapped or challenged children who crave one-on-one attention; volunteering in children's hospital units as clowns, as story readers, as companions when the hurting becomes severe and the fear overwhelms – all turn focus from self to others. All fill a void, not only in the recipient, but also in the giver of the gift. When taking the focus off self and turning to the needs of others, their lives take on meaning, purpose and direction.

It is a simple matter – and often the easiest choice – to sit at home and wallow in self-pity. But Christ in His love wants us to focus on others, to be a servant of His love in a lost and lonely world. *This is how we know what love is: Jesus Christ laid down his life for us. And we ought to lay down our lives for our brothers. If anyone has material possessions and sees his brother in need but has no pity on him, how can the love of God be in him? Dear children, let us not love with words or tongue but with actions and in truth* (1 John 3:16-18).

That laying down of our lives doesn't mean in death, as some perceive. It means giving up our own needs for the needs of others. It is denying self and becoming a servant to all – even those difficult to serve. It means counting all but loss for the overwhelming spiritual supply offered in the process through our Bridegroom. Love, Christ's love, encompasses our very being and an incredible change takes over. We become filled with immeasurable joy, peace and power – those results so often rejected by many for the pleasures of this world.

When that love of Christ fills our very being, we sing for joy. We celebrate His goodness. Discovering the unfailing and continual love supply, we crave and desire more. The more we desire, the more He provides. His unrelenting love knows no end and that love, flowing through us, then becomes unrelenting in us. Priceless, a jewel, sweet to the taste, more precious than gold, we discover a love that knows no end. The supply never runs out. Like the flow of the crystal clear rivers, the Bridegroom's love surges through us with regularity and dependency. Higher than the heavens, deeper than the sea, the unrelenting love of the crucified Savior explodes within.

The only true leader I crave is the Bridegroom, the source of the most incredible love supply to ever encompass my life. And when life thrusts cruel blows on me and I begin to falter, I clinch my fists at the deceiver and shout, "Satan, I will not give up on God. His love is so amazing and so divine. I will trust. I will rely on His source of love – an unrelenting love that knows no bounds. You will not win. Christ is the victor and in Him is my the author and perfector of my faith."

Then my victory cry joins with that of the Apostle Paul in Romans 8:35-39: *Who shall separate us from the love of Christ? Shall trouble or hardship or persecution or famine or nakedness or danger or sword? As it is written: 'For your sake we face death all day long; we are considered as sheep to be slaughtered.' No, in all these things we are more than conquerors through Him who loves us. For I am convinced that neither death nor life, neither angels nor demons, neither the present nor the future, nor any powers, neither height nor depth, nor anything else in all creation, will be able to separate us from the love of God that is in Christ Jesus our Lord.* Amen and amen.

Chapter 13

HIS FULLNESS

Carrots, potatoes and onions appear on my grocery list at least once month. Nutrition from these vegetables supply my body with energy, improve my eyes and leave a lingering taste on the palate.

While the potato tastes rather bland raw, it is wonderfully crunchy. When cooked, baked and grilled, along with butter, salt and pepper, it produces a favorite dish – especially when loaded down with gravy. The carbohydrates energize but, if eaten in too large quantities, can expand the gut beyond my desired measurement. A good thing, overdone, can be a problem.

The carrots contain vitamins and nutrients noted for improvement of the eyes. Shredded they make a wonderful cake. Eaten raw, they become even tastier when used with dips and in salads. Cooked they become especially flavorful after adding a tablespoon of brown sugar. Not only good for you, they are indescribably delicious.

The onion, pungent on the breath, flavors food, enhances salads, and creates a scrumptious hamburger sandwich. I even love to indulge in onion sandwiches, which includes a slice of onion, lots of ketchup and two slices of bread. That proves enough lunch for me – but to the rest of the family, the potent after-effects are not generally welcomed.

There is one important aspect of any of these vegetables. When part of a meal, they bring about a full stomach. When pinched with lack of funds, an onion sandwich eaten on thrift-store bread costs little. It fills my stomach and I am satisfied.

Fried or mashed potatoes with lots of butter eaten with one egg, satisfies my grumbling stomach and costs little. Although I crave it, my mind says, "No, eat a salad instead," or I pay the price in pounds.

And the carrots are tasty anytime, especially during those long lapses between meals. They help me resist my forbidden snack (yet favorite one), chocolate-covered peanuts. I must weigh the balances

– health or pounds. Carrots, a reliable source of energy and nutrients, must be chosen, for they fill me up and grant me a feeling of satisfaction.

How wonderful to be satisfied! When my belly is full, it calms my troubled nerves, settles the rumbling stomach and satisfies the hunger pinch. How wonderful to enjoy carrots, potatoes and onions – all nutritious and filling! Yet the filling does not last. Tomorrow, I will need to make those choices again; carrots or chocolate-covered peanuts, baked potato without sour cream and butter or mashed potatoes and gravy, onion mixed in a salad or a strong-smelling onion sandwich. How I fill my belly is dependent on choices, just as are the choices I make in my life. As I can enlarge my belly with the wrong choices of food, so I can enlarge my self-life with the needless, temporary decisions that create permanent, less satisfying outcomes. Both choices can fill me inwardly, but I must ask: will the end result be temporary and short-lived or eternal and permanent.

The Greatest Filling On Earth

She sat quietly in the doctor's office wondering about the results of tests taken earlier. The pounding in her chest became so loud that she could not help but wonder if others heard. While fearing the worst, she wanted to trust. She knew the goodness of the Lord and desired to be at peace. Yet that dreaded word – cancer – came bounding back into her mind over and over.

The lingering delays and waiting nearly drove her crazy. "Dear God," she cried, "give me the courage to rely on Your strength. I need You more than ever." Then, hearing the nurse call her name, she jumped with a start, realizing the prognosis was only a few moments away.

As she sat quietly in the small examining room, she closed her eyes to center her thoughts on Jesus. She knew He not only knew the results, but would prepare her heart for it. "Jesus, I trust You. Assure me of Your presence. Show me what I need to learn through this. I feel so weak."

Within an instant, the door opened and her doctor entered. Sitting before her, he first made small talk, which would normally have caused a reaction of inner screams from her. But this time, there were no inner screams – just a calmness and quietness she had not experienced earlier. When he finally approached the subject of her tests, she noticed little apprehension – she knew she was ready for the results.

Her blood pressure remained normal. Her heart beat normally. His words, though difficult, soothed her like a mother's tender touch. "There is cancer but it is very slight. Appearing to be in its beginning stages, I believe we can remove it successfully with surgery. If you hadn't noticed the abnormality until later, there is no telling how bad it could have gotten. We must truly be thankful for small miracles."

As her tears flowed, she inwardly rejoiced, not only at the results, but at the overwhelming embrace that she felt from her precious Bridegroom. He was there for her. She experienced Him within and without. She rested in the fact that not only was she in Him, but He in her. How could she lose, no matter what was ahead! He loved her beyond measure and she knew it. Welcoming a remembered Psalm in her mind, she prayed, "You have filled my heart with greater joy than when their grain and new wine abound. I will lie down and sleep in peace, for you alone, O Lord, make me dwell in safety" (Psalm 4:7-8).

One of the most beautiful Psalms in the Bible, memorized by many is the 23rd Psalm. Comforting to the spirit in all types of circumstances, it assures many of His divine presence in the midst of trying and difficult events. However, there is one phrase that took on new meaning for me as I was preparing this chapter. Using the King James Version of the Bible, through which I memorized this Psalm, the phrase my cup runneth over exemplifies the eternal goodness of the

Lord. Filling us to overflowing with all of Himself, there is no limit to His strength, His power, His love, His goodness, and His faithfulness. Filled to overflowing, our cup truly overflows with every desire He imagines for us. It overflows with abundant treasures beyond comprehension (Psalm 23:5).

Difficult to imagine is the overwhelming person of God. No matter what our mind can conjure up, He exceeds that and more. However wide our perspective of His abilities, it is greater. The depths of despair cannot escape His boundless love, nor can the heights of heaven surpass it. He sheds all His goodness to everyone even though not everyone receives and accepts it with joy.

The loving Bridegroom will move every mountain, swim every ocean, and undertake every task to reveal His all-consuming love and passion for us. Whether it be in our moments of despair or our most ecstatic moment, He moves into our lives in silent ways, in powerful ways and through the lives of others, simply to say, "I love you. I want you for My own. Please heed the invitation. Listen to My voice. Then My Spirit, in all His power and presence, will walk you through the door to My fullness – My amazing spiritual joy."

Christ In Us

Fullness consists in His presence in us. Once we acknowledge the power of Christ in our lives and yield to Him, He fills us to overflowing. It spills over into the lives of others and remains as a never-ending source of supply. He pines to hold us close and to pour out His Spirit into our hearts. Through it, He displays His lavishness of wealth at our fingertips. Not understanding that giving up the things of this life yields His superabundance of heavenly gifts and fruit, we squelch His goodness by refusing to yield ourselves to Him.

Because of His passionate need to bring us into His fold and to fill our cup to overflowing, He displayed the extreme in passion. His passion on the cross of Calvary carried your sins and mine. It erased the guilt forever burdening our hearts. It freed us to serve the living God in a manner only understood in His presence. It announces a depth of love for us beyond comprehension. Through His sacrifice and resurrection, He trumpets a release from the bondage of Satan and the victory found only in Him.

John tells us in his first letter, *This is love: not that we loved God, but that he loved us and sent his Son as an atoning sacrifice for our sins. Dear friends, since God so loved us, we also ought to love one another. No one has ever seen God; but if we love one another, God lives in us and his love is made compete in us* (1 John 4:10-12).

Living in that love we absorb His love, His fullness. *For in Christ all the fullness of the Deity lives in bodily form, and you have been give fullness in Christ* (Colossians 2:9-10a). Women, can you imagine! Christ lives in us. He fills us to overflowing. We now have His fullness embedded in our spirits, willing to revitalize, re-energize and reactivate our weary, worn spirits. Believe it! Claim it! Enjoy it!

We Live In Him

Only half of the equation is present in the above title. Leaving this step out is like saying that one half makes a whole. Think of yourself as an empty glass. As Christ's power enters our spirit, He fills that glass to the brim. His presence is in you.

Now take that glass of water, place it into a clear, glass pitcher and continue to pour. As it overflows into the pitcher and fills it, you understand better how you are in Christ and He is in you. The amazing result and blessing is when we look at it and realize that there is not one area in which we are not totally encased in His love. Forever present, forever abundant, we cannot escape from that love. His fullness (represented by the water) totally surrounds us – inside and out.

John again says, *If anyone acknowledges that Jesus is the Son of God, God lives in him and he in God. And so we know and rely on the love God has for us. God is love. Whoever lives in love lives in God, and God in him* (1 John 4:15-16). How, then, can we not be filled with His fullness? As we grasp the extent of His love, as we bathe ourselves in His flood of cleansing blood, and as we believe in the active participation of the Holy Spirit, we also realize that we are *filled to all the measure of all the fullness of God* (Ephesians 3:19). It is all-consuming and all-encompassing. Accept it as real and active. Celebrate His goodness as He fills you to overflowing.

O Lord, you have searched me and you know me. You know when I sit and when I rise; you perceive my thoughts from afar. You discern my going out and my lying down; you are familiar with all my ways. Before a word is on my tongue you know it completely, O Lord. You hem me in – behind and before; you have laid your hand upon me. Such knowledge is too wonderful for me, too lofty for me to attain. Where can I go from your Spirit? Where can I flee from your presence? If I go up to the heavens, you are there; if I make my bed in the depths, you are there. If I rise on the wings of the dawn, if I settle on the far side of the sea, even there your hand will guide me, your right hand will hold me fast (Psalm 139:1-10).

"Help me, dear Bridegroom, to acknowledge Your presence in and around me. May I never lose sight of Your amazing love. Amen."

Chapter 14

ETERNAL LIFE

How do you describe it? In what expanse of words do you portray an eternal God, eternal purposes, eternal love, eternal power and eternal desires? No matter the extent of gratitude I feel inside, the constant emergence of descriptive words available just don't seem adequate. Yet, in reality they can all be summed up in two words – Jesus Christ.

As floodwaters cover the earth, so His gentle Spirit floods our spirits with His goodness. As the giant whale submerges into the depths of the sea, His compassion, His strength and His forgiveness dives deeply into our hearts. When the events of this life swallow us up as a snake swallows a small rodent, He carefully wraps us in an eternity of faithfulness and unrelenting, steadfast love, assuring us of His protection. Grasping us with His right hand of power, the Bridegroom holds tightly while keeping His eye on the Father with an interceding eye, in hopes that we will listen to His call for surrender, submission and trust. The ache inside weighs heavily. The tears flow endlessly. Desiring that none should perish, He plans our lives and the lives of our loved ones in such a way that everyone everywhere, who desires His presence, may be lead to the truth. Oh, the joy when a child turns to Him and says, "Yes, Jesus, I desire to have You as my Bridegroom. Yes, dear Jesus, I desire to follow the will of my Father, just as You did. Yes, dear Jesus, send me Your Holy Spirit, that I may be full to overflowing with all the eternal blessings and pleasures at Your right hand. I want You – all of You, for You are eternal life."

That is when the windows of heaven open. Angels rejoice, singing praises in heaven; tears of sadness replaced by tears of eternal joy. Another child enters eternal life – not only forever as an inheritance, but today – now – in the presence and power of Jesus Christ who is *the way and the truth and the life* (John 14:6).

But the tears of anguish and agony when one fails to heed His call forever burdens His heart, so filled with love. The nailing to the cross continues in His very being as He experiences rejection again and again. That pain never goes away. In anguish, He cries, "Why won't they believe that everything I did was for them? Can't they see that the torture, the torment, the rejection, the suffering, the anguish, the physical pain, the spiritual torment in hell, and the final resurrection were all for them. My love so deep, My desire so strong, and My joy set before Me absorbed every step I took. My Father assured Me it was the only way and, for Him and for them, I willingly endured. Why? I knew the final result – eternal life – both now and forever. Please take heed, dear friends. Please come to Me. My hands, scarred as a reminder of that love, reach out daily. I will wait – for the rest of your life."

Life Is In His Son

And this is the testimony: God has given us eternal life, and this life is in his Son. He who has the Son has life; he who does not have the Son of God does not have life. I write these things to you who believe in the name of the Son of God so that you may know that you have eternal life...We know also that the Son of God has come and has given us understanding, so that we may know him who is true. And we are in him who is true – even in his Son Jesus Christ. He is the true God and eternal life (1 John 5:11-13,20).

One cannot inherit the presence and power of Jesus Christ without also inheriting eternal life. When, through His Holy Spirit, He takes residence in you, all His eternal pleasures and powers abide in you as well. If I were to list them, when would it end? All that is goodness, once wrapped in swaddling cloths, now abides in the highest heavens and sits at the right hand of the throne of God, His Father. Once nailed on a cross in shame, He is now worshipped and adored. And one day in the future, the resurrected Christ will see every knee bow and every tongue confess that He is Lord, to the glory of God the Father (Philippians 2:10-11). He is the eternal Lord. He is the righteous King. He is all we need and He will supply us with His abundance in the eternal realm.

Yet, in this encumbered life, we believe that eternal life is only a future event. The monotony, the temptations, the wonders of the world, and the long-time waiting, all break down our will to listen and to believe that eternal life is ours today. In this world of quick fix, fast food, and instant reply, we want all the gusto – here and now. Believing in inner peace but wanting our wish list filled today, we wash the hope of His abiding, eternal presence down the drain. Eternity is too far away. We want our **desires** met – and right now!

Unfortunately, with attitudes and actions that reflect that thinking, the eternal presence of the living Christ remains beyond our experience and enjoyment. We allow the outward signs of pleasure to fill our cups. The Bridegroom experiences rejection as we reply, "I want what I want, when I want it."

Hatred abounds. Selfishness settles in our families, our churches, and our schools. The very fiber of our lives shatters and shakes. Instead of bringing satisfaction, the short-term pleasures create a hunger for more – bigger houses, fancier clothes, sportier cars, and the most modern of anything and everything. Unrestrained by our pleasures, our credit cards bulge with debt, our home loans exceed hundreds of thousands of dollars and the three or more cars reflect enormous payments. Satisfied with less, we accumulate more, and more is what we get – more debt, more greed, more unhappiness. Could there be something to contentment in Christ? Are His eternal pleasures worth seeking?

You have made known to me the path of life; you will fill me with joy in your presence, with eternal pleasures at your right hand (Psalm 16:11).

Will we ever listen? Will we ever truly believe?

What's In It For Me?

Scrubbing the floors on my hands and knees is a position I hate, yet also love. The scrubbing and the aching knees serve as reminders of work – hard work. But the results of a shiny floor, void of dirt in the corners and cracks, grants me the reward of a job well done – in spite of the discomforts.

I believe that nothing worthwhile comes easily. Often the more pain required in accomplishing the finished product, the more enjoyable the outcome. Just as scrubbing brings about shiny, clean floors, so the scrubbing of our spirits brings about polished, beloved children of faith. The painful circumstances, the prolonged waiting on the Lord, and the powerful message of love in the midst of our difficulties forever builds up our spirits and nourishes our hungry souls.

When we wait, when we succumb in trust, when we search for Him as for silver, what's in it for us? Exactly what will we receive that is so amazing and so divine that we will give up everything for Him?

We receive nothing other than Jesus Christ Himself – the ultimate reward. Through the power of the Holy Spirit, our eyes open to the truths enclosed in Scripture and His amazing eternity of blessings overflow. As we give and yield more and more to Him, more and more of Him will surface. Our attitudes change. Our desires center not in self, but in Him. The hunger and thirst for this life appear less important and the sharing of Him surges deeply. The changes cannot be understood but they happen. The old world cravings disappear, replaced by cravings of inner peace. Failing to fully understand before, a desire to do the Father's will and seek His presence dominates. The more of Him we seek, the less of the world we desire. The eternal pleasures and joy flow in and the old selfishness flows out. Christ, our Bridegroom, changes us. The amazing grace of His Spirit transforms our wearied spirits. Now we crave the eternal purpose and pleasures found only in Christ. Joy escalates. Praise dominates. A willingness to give thanks for His abiding love and comfort in the midst of the circumstances dominates our will and desire. To God be the glory! He creates the change. He opens the window of eternity here and now – for eternal life is Christ. In Him, we possess eternal life for He is in us and we are in Him.

After Jesus said this, he looked toward heaven and prayed: 'Fa-

ther, the time has come. Glorify Your Son, that Your Son may glorify You. For You granted Him authority over all people that He might give eternal life to all those You have given Him. Now this is eternal life: That they may know You, the only true God, and Jesus Christ, whom You have sent…I have made You known to them, and will continue to make You known in order that the love You have for Me may be in them and that I Myself may be in them' (John 17:1-3,26).

So what do we get out of it anyway? While the Source of eternal pleasures can only be physically viewed upon our return to heaven, eternal pleasures flow from our Bridegroom today. They include: diligence, compassion, strong work ethic, wisdom, a radiant life, purity, reverence, gentleness, a quiet spirit, freedom from fear, a trusting heart, an unrelenting love, His fullness, peace, joy, faithfulness, self-control, deliverance, perseverance, unfailing love, His righteousness, a forgiving heart, pleasant boundaries, His strength, guidance, and eternal life.

Discover the endless supply of eternal joy and pleasures in Him. Seek Him in His Word, wherein lies all the hidden treasures of eternal life! Find comfort in the Father's presence, pray for the filling of the Spirit, and embrace joyfully your precious Bridegroom, Jesus Christ.

Listen to the powerful words of promise made by King David to his son Solomon: *And you, my son Solomon, acknowledge the God of your father, and serve Him with wholehearted devotion and with a willing mind, for the Lord searches every heart and understands every motive behind the thoughts. If you seek Him, He will be found by you* (1 Chronicles 28:9). Seek your Bridegroom and He will be found by you. That is His promise!

Our Future Inheritance

And God raised us up with Christ and seated us with him in the heavenly realms in Christ Jesus, in order that in the coming age he might show the incomparable riches of his grace, expressed in his kindness to us in Christ Jesus (Ephesians 2:6-7).

An eternity of grace – available now and in the future. As we revel in the eternal pleasures at His right hand provided to us now, one day at a time, we also look forward with eager expectation, its fulfillment.

Death maintains no hold on us. Christ broke the chains of death and we have victory – over death and the grave. We possess life everlasting – without end. Though a time of sleep is inevitable, in our eyes it is only an instant. As Jesus cradles our souls in His heavenly realms, our bodies decay. But in a twinkling of an eye, the eternal life we experience today becomes complete, joyous, ecstatic, and forever. What wondrous anticipation the saints in the past felt in that knowledge!

While we below mourn the loss of our loved ones, often agonizingly so, it must not be for them. I can only imagine my first husband, my sister, my loving grandparents, my parents and a stillborn grandchild cradled in an enormity of Love – far beyond our comprehension. It is what He destined for them. It was part of His plan of love to eventually embrace them and us, in due time, with all the generous, incredible blessings of eternity – wrapped in one moment of time. Does it make their passing any less important or any less painful. No! But their work for which He sent them was stamped with the word "Completed!" Whatever the age span, or circumstances prior to their death, or the pain incurred by me after their death, they completed their heaven-sent labors for Christ. Now they rest in the loving, compassionate hands of their eternal Savior, where they will remain secure until I view them again, never to be removed from their presence – ever!

I once heard the story of a man who died on the operating table. Through the concentrated and diligent efforts of doctors and nurses, he revived. Upon discovering his after-death experience, many questioned the events that took place. His reply was, "If you can imagine the most ecstatic event in your life and magnify it 100 times, it could not even come close to the joys that await us in heaven."

Eternal life is our inheritance. It awaits all who trust in the divine person of Jesus Christ. Those that seek Him, abide in Him, and relish His eternal pleasures here will be overwhelmed. They will shout, "It doesn't get any better than this!"

Jesus said, *I tell you the truth, whoever hears my word and believes him who sent me has eternal life and will not be condemned; he has crossed over from death to life* (John 5:24).

Do not work for food that spoils, but food that endures to eternal life, which the Son of Man will give. On him God the Father has placed his seal of approval...For my Father's will is that everyone who looks to the Son and believes him shall have eternal life, and I will raise him up at the last day (John 6:27,49). Amen and Amen!

Chapter Bible Studies

Chapter 1 — DILIGENCE

The Proverbs 31 woman always appeared to me as a threat. How could anyone possibly match her qualities? With the strength of an ox, the diligence of an ant, and the knowledge of a philosopher, she accomplished impossible feats and did incredible deeds. My meager efforts did not hold a candle to hers.

Yet in time, I learned to realize that growth in these areas occur as surely as the sun shines. In seeking His Word, I discovered traits I knew could not rest in me.

In verse 30, the power source for the Proverbs 31 woman appears. Read the verse and then complete the sentence below.

"Charm is deceptive, and beauty is fleeting; but a woman _______

____."

Left on our own, the toils and the efforts assigned to us can become drudgery. With routines, harried schedules, and overwhelming demands, we often feel stretched to the limits.

But God wants to change something in the heart of it all. In striving to do His will, His way with His supply, He opens our hearts to the powerful, diligent Spirit within. Given as a gift from the Bridegroom, we seek Him in His Word and discover the positive effects of diligence in our work.

Ecclesiastes reveals several negative reasons for diligence in our toiling. Read the following sections. List those aspects.

Ecclesiastes 4:48 ____

____

Ecclesiastes 5:10 ____

____

Ecclesiastes 6:3,7 ____

____

The prodding, pushing, exhausting energies expended wear on us daily – and for what? Until we recognize the meaninglessness of selfish toil and accept the Christ-like diligence found only in Him, joy will not surface. Read and study the following passages to understand the differences.

Ecclesiastes 2:24-26

Ecclesiastes 3:11-14

Ecclesiastes 5:18-20

Romans 12:11

Ephesians 6:7-8

Colossians 3:23-24

Accepting God's role in our lives, we turn to Him for more than strength to "do what we want to do." Rather, we daily surrender to His goodness, offer ourselves as living sacrifices in accomplishing His will, and seek His guidance in the process. Then turning to His Spirit, we pray for His Christ-like diligence – the diligence manifested on the road to the cross.

In doing so, mighty miracles occur. Read again of the Proverbs 31 woman as you discover the awesome tasks accomplished through a God-fearing woman. List those tasks. Then relate how they can apply to your labors, when done in Christ's power. What mighty things would you like to do for Him?

verse 13 ______________________________

____

verse 14 ______________________________

____

verse 15 ______________________________

____

verse 16 ______________________________

____

verse 17 ______________________________

____

verses 18-19 ______________________________

____

Diligent efforts centered on a diligent God produce diligent service. As you focus on your varied ministries in Christ, turn to Him as an example and an ongoing source of divine comfort. Read Hebrews 12:2-3 for that example.

As Jesus *resolutely* set His face toward Jerusalem, knowing it would end at the cross of Calvary, so we consider that kind of love when serving others with diligence (Luke 9:51). Remember: "When

God gives us a course of action, we must move steadily toward our destination, no matter what potential hazards await us there."[5]

With Christ as your Guide, may He serve as your loving example of strength and diligence as you accomplish the tasks He has called you to do.

PRAYER: Jesus, My Bridegroom, I praise and thank You for the love that continued to move ever forward to the cross. Give me the strength to turn my eyes upon You whenever the going gets tough and the stress overwhelms. Keep me centered on Your love and Your power as I diligently strive to fulfill the Father's will. In Your name I pray. Amen.

Chapter 2 — COMPASSION

She stood at the grave-side coffin looking at the faces of her four young children. Unable to grasp the reason for his death, she screamed inwardly, "Father, how will we make it? What is going to happen to us now?" Suddenly without warning, a small cloud covered the sun and a shower of light rain ensued. Looking upward, she noticed that in the midst of a clear blue sky, only one cloud existed. With tears in her eyes, she smiled and said, "God understands my pain. He is crying with me."

Christ, our Bridegroom, does express and reveal His compassion to us in times of grief. His heart feels the burdens in our hearts and it moves Him to respond. As you read the following examples of His compassion, take note of the action He provided.

Matthew 9:35-36 ______________________________

____

Matthew 14:13-14 ______________________________

____

Matthew 20:34 ______________________________

____

Mark 1:40-42 ______________________________

____

Luke 7:13 ______________________________

____

Luke 15:20 ____

____

Luke 19:41 ____

____

John 11:33-35 ____

____

That compassion is still available to us today. As His generous heart of compassion and love spills into our lives, He desires that we share that compassion with others. Read 2 Corinthians 1:1-3.

Encountering and maturing in Christ through the death of a spouse, parent, or child, we support the hurting hearts of others in their similar struggles. Overcoming, with Christ's help, the ravages of abuse, drug or alcohol addiction or fears beyond measure, we can compassionately reach out to others who seek our guidance and comfort. As we *clothe ourselves with compassion*, His generating love and compassion flows through to others (Colossians 3:12). Use the following verses for guidelines in seeking wisdom and guidance.

Philippians 2:1-2

Ephesians 4:32

Colossians 3:12

1 Peter 3:8

Then there is that example given to us in the Proverbs 31 woman – that super-human woman who runs circles around us. What a dynamic example this God-fearing woman is to us! As you read Proverbs 31:20, name the ways she revealed her compassion to others.

Whether to the poor and needy, to the grieving and despairing, or to the destitute and lost – all need compassion. We are to become the vessels through which He is revealed. Absorbing the promises of compassion in His Word, we inhale it with the intent of exhaling it into the lives of others.

The following verses aid us in our growth and understanding of the compassion that originates in the heart of God. Read them carefully as you rest in His goodness and love.

Isaiah 30:18

Isaiah 49:10,13

Isaiah 54:10

Lamentations 3:22-23

Psalm 51:1

Psalm 90:13-14

Psalm 111:4-5

Psalm 116:5

Rejoice in the gift of love and compassion given to you as you grant comfort in abundance to others.

PRAYER: Jesus, for Your divine holy love, I praise You. For Your tender compassion, I bow before You. As I gaze at Your eyes, dear Jesus, may I never forget the deepest revelations of compassion and love revealed as You wore the intertwined crown to the cross for me. Grant me the ability to use that gift to minister to others. In Your name I pray. Amen.

Chapter 3 — STRONG WORK ETHIC

"Once Jesus lifts you into God's presence, you are free to obey – out of love, not necessity, and through God's power, not your own. You know that if you stumble, you will not fall to the ground. Instead you will be caught and held in Christ's loving arms."[6]

Hard work should not elude us. The Bridegroom gains pleasure in the accomplished goals of our heart planted by the seed of His love. When granted a vision, one of the greatest gifts we can give Him is the committed, productive fulfillment of that goal He set before us.

Paul tells us that *whoever sows sparingly will also reap sparingly, and whoever sows generously will also reap generously* (2 Corinthians 9:6). The rewards of hard labor for Christ brings satisfaction, joy and pleasure. In addition, He bestows blessings of overabundant supply for the task at hand. As you read the following section regarding those blessings, fill in the missing blanks.

2 Corinthians 9:8,10-11: *And God is able to make ___________ grace abound to you, so that in ___________ things at ___________ times, having ___________ that you need, you will ___________________ in every good work...Now he who ________________________ seed to the sower and bread for food will also___________________ and ________________ your store of seed will ________________ the harvest of your ________________________. You will be made ________________ in ______________________ way so that you can be ________________ on ____________________ occasion,*

and through us your ______________________ *will result in*

______________________ *to God.*

Whatever our giving – time, energy, talents, or money – the Bridegroom plants a strong work ethic into our spirit, which in turn flows out to others. Nothing is impossible to those who listen to His call and fulfill it for His grace and glory.

Read 2 Corinthians 9:12-15 to discover the ultimate outcome of labors done for Christ, our Bridegroom.

Overwhelmed with His goodness as we seek His strength *in* and *through* our labors, Christ supplies the power and supply. Study the following verses as you list how this will be accomplished.

Galatians 6:9-10 ______________________________________

____

Ephesians 3:20-21 ______________________________________

____

Colossians 3:23-24 ______________________________________

____

After completing the study of these sections, ask yourself the following questions. Refer to the following verses for guidance.

1. Am I obedient to His call even if it involves hard work? (Galatians 6:9)

2. Do I rely on myself, void of Christ's power, or do I seek Him first

and accomplish all things through His grace and power? (Ephesians 3:20-21)

3. Do I produce fruitful harvest? (John 15:4)

4. Do I possess a living union with Christ, my Bridegroom, trusting Him for my productiveness and supply? (John 15:5)

5. Is what I do making a contribution to the lives of others? (2 Corinthians 9:12-13)

6. Am I willing to sacrifice my needs out of love for Christ? (Romans 12:1-3 and 2 Corinthians 8:4-5)

Remember: "Good workers take pride in the quality and beauty of their work. God is concerned about the quality and beauty of what you do. Whether you are a corporate executive or a drugstore cashier, your work should reflect the creative abilities God has given you."[7]

PRAYER: Jesus, I praise and thank You for the privilege of possessing a strong work ethic from You. Alone, my labors are selfish and in vain. In and with You, my labors make sense, create joy, and produce abundant blessings for others. Hold me close as I daily seek strength from Your Spirit, pursuing only those labors that bring honor and glory to You. In Your precious name I pray. Amen.

Chapter 4 — WISDOM

Our life often seems shadowed. Knowing we should experience power, we feel helpless. Desiring strength, weakness reigns. Expecting peace, fear and inner struggles boggle our minds. We ask, "Why can't I acquire the spiritual blessings promised? What is the missing key that unlocks His strength and power in my life?"

Crying out for His strength, we begin to understand that wisdom can unlock the windows of heaven. Recognizing Christ as our true Wisdom, we turn to the power found in Scripture and in His presence. As you read Proverbs 2:1-4 list the steps vital to our search for wisdom. Notice the intensity of the action verb in each statement.

1. ______________________ my words

2. ______________________ my commands

3. __________________ your ______________ to wisdom

4. __________________ your _________________ to understanding

5. ____________________ ____________________ for insight

6. ____________________ _________________ for understanding

7. __________________ for it as for ___________________

8. __________________ for it as for ___________________

Searching for wisdom in the midst of the mundane, the ordinary, the confusing, and the grieving experiences often demands intense, dedicated commitment to the seeking of His will and way. Believing a rescue is already taking place, we praise Him for granting us His wisdom. As praise fills our page, the fulfillment of our search pours into our lives. Continue reading Proverbs 2 and list the rich rewards for seeking wisdom, understanding and insight.

verse 5 ______________________________________

verse 6 ______________________________________

verse 7 ______________________________________

verse 8 ______________________________________

Verse 6 clearly states the source of wisdom. Who is that source? How is that further elaborated on in the following verses?

Colossians 2:3
Romans 11:33-36
1 Corinthians 1:23-24,30-31

Absorb the realization that only in Christ, the True Key, can we attain true wisdom – to face the daily struggles, to conquer the negative attitudes, and to heal the grieving spirit. As we fix our hearts on Him, His truths spill over into our inner being. His power, love and wisdom replace the mixed-up existence we experience. He alone revives, nourishes, and changes us – but only as we focus on Him, believing all wisdom comes from Him.

There is one detrimental obstacle to our search for wisdom. As you read James 1:5-7, name the promise and the obstacle.

promise ____

____

obstacle ____

____

Believe and don't doubt! Wisdom is promised – **He** is promised. Jesus, your precious Bridegroom **is** wisdom. Look for Him as for silver and search for Him as for hidden treasure.

Close this study by reading Proverbs 3:13-18. Substitute the word "Jesus" for "wisdom" and the words "He/Him" for "she/her". Discover Christ anew!

PRAYER: Dear Jesus, I know You are true wisdom. You possess all the treasures of heaven and I have only to seek You to discover them. As I fall before You on bended knee, supply me with the wisdom in You I crave. Grant that through You and in You, I may be clothed with strength and dignity and may laugh at the days to come. Enable me to speak with Your wisdom as I reveal Your goodness to others. Amen.

Chapter 5 — RADIANCE

Husbands, love your wives, just as Christ loved the church and gave himself up for her, to make her holy, cleansing her by the washing with water through the word, and to present her to himself as a radiant church, without stain or wrinkle or any other blemish, but holy and blameless (Ephesians 5:25-27).

Some adjectives that can be used to describe radiance include: serene, glaring, rapturous, reflected, celestial, soft, blinding, indescribable, warm, splendid, resplendent, glorious, and gleaming. Synonyms include: brilliant, bright, luminous, beaming, and lucent.

What a precious gift He gives us! Because of His great love for us, our lives emit His glory. Emblazoned and empowered by Him, we enter His presence as a radiant bride, without stain, wrinkle or blemish. Even the vilest offender, when covered with Christ, is cleansed. We appear before the throne of grace as holy and blameless, washed with the waters of baptism and the shed blood of Christ. Then, standing in His grace alone, we glow, we radiate, and we are resplendent.

The radiance of Christ flows into our lives. A transformation to higher glory takes place. Read 2 Corinthians 3:7-18 and answer the following questions:

1. Why did Moses veil his face? (verse 13)
2. From whom did the radiance come? (See Exodus 34:29)
3. Who alone can remove the veil to reveal the radiance? (verse 14b, 16)
4. When we receive the power of the Spirit, what transformation takes place? (verse 18)

Standing firm in Christ, we radiate the Spirit's power to others. How is this done according to the following verses?

John 8:12
2 Corinthians 1:21-22
2 Corinthians 2:14-15
2 Corinthians 4:6-11,16-18
2 Corinthians 5:14-21
Ephesians 5:8-9
1 John 1:5-7

When we reflect Christ's radiance, are we aware of it? Probably not (See Exodus 24:9). Yet we who see God's glory cannot but reflect that glory. Dwelling in His presence on a regular basis, through fellowship in the body, the Word, prayer, and the Lord's Supper, we display a radiance only He can give.

David and others in the Psalms understood the glory of God and the obvious revelation of His light. As you look up the following verses, record the statement that indicates that fact.

Psalm 4:6b ______________________________

____

Psalm 44:3 ______________________________

____

Psalm 76:4 ______________________________

____

Psalm 89:15 ______________________________

____

Psalm 104:1-2 ____

____

Psalm 118:27a ____

____

Arise and shine, ye peoples of God, for your Light has come. Your Bridegroom desires to reveal His glory to you. Pray that He may open your eyes to Christ as He transforms you into His likeness, filling you to the measure of all the fullness of God.

PRAYER: Holy Father, what a privilege to be a human reflector of Your Son. Open my eyes to His love and glory in my life and flood my soul with His Spirit. Give me courage to reflect that gospel light with others so that I may point them to Christ, the true Light of love. In His name, I pray. Amen.

Chapter 6 — PURITY

As He looked into her eyes, He saw the loneliness and the emptiness. Feeling inwardly dirty because of past sins, she couldn't imagine anyone loving her. Yet He saw what she could become and, as her eyes lifted in submission to Him, He poured His purity over her. No longer smothered with guilt and shame, she now took on the pure washing of an abiding love that would last through all eternity. What joy filled her soul! What pride filled His!

Jesus **is** the Lover of our souls. He pours His purity over our guilt-ridden, sin-filled lives. As we acknowledge His forgiveness and accept His all-surpassing love, our hearts soften to His touch and our broken spirits revive.

As you read Hebrews 10:19-23, answer the following questions:

1. According to verse 19, what is the only way we can have confidence in entering the "Most Holy Place" – the place where God dwells?

2. When we, with a sincere heart, draw near to God, we are assured of ____

   ____. (verse 22)

3. How sure can we be that this cleansing and washing with His pure water will occur? (verse 23)

Christ promises to present us to the Father as His pure bride. As He draws us, His bride, to Himself, He makes us holy, cleansing us by the washing with water through the Word. He presents us to the Father without stain, wrinkle or blemish. In His eyes and in the

Father's eyes, we are pure. How did He accomplish this?

Ephesians 5:25
Philippians 2:5-8
Colossians 1:13-14,19-20
Hebrews 7:25-27
Hebrews 9:11-14

Hebrews 9:14 says: *How much more, then, will the blood of Christ who through the eternal Spirit offered himself unblemished to God, cleanse our consciences from acts that lead to death, so that we may serve the living God.*

Write again the words that follow "so" ______________________

____

We are saved "from" but called "to". Our reaction to His purity is loving, heart-felt, obedient service. In the following verses, record what each says regarding that reaction.

Proverbs 20:11 ______________________________________

____

Philippians 1:9-11 ___________________________________

____

Philippians 2:14-16a _________________________________

____

1 Timothy 1:5 _______________________________________

____

James 1:27 ____

____

Cry with David, *Create in me a pure heart, O God, and renew a steadfast spirit within me* (Psalm 51:10). Hold fast to your Bridegroom's faithfulness and forever claim the righteousness that comes only from Him. With dedicated hearts, lift your eyes to Him in surrender and open your arms to others in service.

PRAYER: Holy Father, I stand before Your throne of grace covered in the blood of Jesus Christ. Hear my plea for mercy and wash me with Your assurance of forgiveness, purity, and grace. As I turn my eyes toward Jesus, may His love ever motivate and move me into loving service for others. In His name, I pray. Amen.

Chapter 7 — A REVERENT SPIRIT

No one questioned her love for Him. It was obvious as she maintained a close, intimate relationship with her Bridegroom. Not only reflecting honor and awe, she demonstrated a deep abiding reverence for the One she trusted and obeyed. And it seemed, the more difficult her circumstances, the deeper her love became. There was no mistaking the genuineness of her unique, devoted heart.

Psalm 84:10-12 helps us to view what lies at the heart of this reverent woman. As she cries, "I am content with You," she realizes that Jesus, her Bridegroom is enough. All else seems insignificant.

So it is with any woman whose heart has been touched by the Master. Not only does she desire to spend time with Him but also craves to offer praise and thanksgiving to Him for who He is and what He has done.

In order to develop a heart close to God, we must trust Him to draw us into an intimate relationship with Himself – and He promises He will. But time must be spent in His Word, where His goodness is revealed. As you look up the following verses in Psalm 119, record what glories and pleasures await you there.

verse 9 ____

____

verse 14 ____

____

verse 18 ____

____

verse 24 ____

____

verse 28 ____

____

verse 32 ____

____

verse 43 ____

____

verse 52 ____

____

verse 72 ____

____

verse 77 ____

____

verse 93 ____

____

verses 99, 100 ____

____

verse 105 ____

____

verse 114 ____

____

verse 125 ____

____

verse 135 ____

____

verse 165 ____

____

Our outward result: verses 171, 172 ____________________

____

Now list ways you can avail yourself to Him and His grace and mercy. The following references will help you.

Psalm 63:7
Psalm 86:11
Isaiah 26:8-9
Isaiah 55:6
Jeremiah 33:3
Hebrews 12:1-3
James 3:8,10

In so doing, He promises to revitalize you through His Spirit. See Isaiah 58:10b-11 and Titus 3:4-8. Also, Isaiah 40:31 assures us that *those who hope in the Lord will renew their strength. They will soar on wings like eagles; they will run and not grow weary, they will walk and not be faint.* Renewed in His strength and hope, we fall before Him in adoration and praise.

Use Psalm 145 as your closing hymn of praise, for He is deserving of all honor and glory.

PRAYER: Holy, precious Jesus, You have been my example of love, honor and praise. Open my eyes to the gracious, tenderhearted love You give to me and for the power I can receive only through You. As I kneel before You in humbleness of heart, draw me into Your presence once more so that I may evermore revere Your holy name – the name that is above every name in heaven, on earth and under the earth. Amen.

Chapter 8 — GENTLENESS

And the Bridegroom said to His Father, "Give her the unfading beauty of a gentle and quiet spirit, which is of greater value in our sight. Nothing can compare. Nothing reveals My love more. As I shed My light upon her, may that gentleness that flows in and through Me be evident to all."

In today's world, women are expected to be strong, domineering, and controlling. Unless they portray the liberated woman, they are considered bound.

Yet I maintain that the truly free woman is the one who finds her rest, her quietness in the heart of her Savior. Clasping tightly to His heart of tender grace, she discovers a release of the claims of this world. Secure in Him, she knows her security and power rest in His goodness. All the troubles and cares of this life find release in a manner unaccepted by most.

As we study Scripture, let us view God's gentleness and learn how that gentleness is molded and shaped within us.

In the Old Testament, God did not always confront His people with thunder and lightening or in a cloud and pillar of fire. As you read 1 Kings 19:9-12, discover how He approached Elijah at a low point in his life.

He still confronts us in that manner today. In the quiet devotional times, Jesus calms our troubled spirits. In all gentleness, He assures us of His presence and soothes the fears.

As you read the following references, record how He describes Himself.

Matthew 21:3-5 ____

____

Matthew 11:28-30 ____

____

Paul also describes His tenderness through humility in Philippians 2:6-8 ____

____

In 2 Corinthians 10:1-6, Paul referred to the gentleness and meekness of Christ as being demonstrated within himself. For what reason did he call upon those inner qualities? Based on these verses, does gentleness and meekness imply cowardice or a "mousy" attitude?

Speaking up for what we believe to be true in Christ takes courage and strength. Paul used divine power to demolish strongholds. He was ready to punish acts that lead to disobedience.

So, too, we must in all gentleness and tenderness, stand up for what we believe to be true. As you read the following verses, list the guidelines for doing so.

Ephesians 4:14-15
Colossians 3:16-17
Colossians 4:5-6
1 Corinthians 10:23-24, 31-33

When Christ, through His Spirit, convicts us in tenderness and gentleness, He portrays a Bridegroom who always has our best interest at heart. It is never for selfish gain or gratification. His amazing love washes over the vilest offender and then, creates within a love like His that also loves others in gentleness and tenderness – yet proves to be bold and courageous.

Read the following verses. Then list the inner changes that take place through Him.

1 Corinthians 4:20-21
Ephesians 4:2
Colossians 3:10,12
1 Timothy 6:11b,12a
1 Peter 4:15

As you conclude this Bible study, dwell on the greatest gifts we can give to others through the power of Christ within us.

Philippians 2:1-4
2 Corinthians 5:14-17

PRAYER: Dear precious Jesus, as I rest my weary soul on You, I pray for Your Spirit's power. In that power, give me the courage to speak of Your truth in love but to do so with Your gentleness and tenderness. Never let me forget the grace given to me that washed over a multitude of sins, that I may in turn cover the multitude of sins for others with Your love. In Your name, I pray. Amen.

Chapter 9 — QUIET SPIRIT

With pointed finger aimed at her, he hurled insults in anger. Lies flowed from his mouth, reflecting his low self-esteem. Frustrated that he couldn't maintain support and control at work, he discovered it easier to attack her rather than admit his own failures and insecurities.

Struggling with hurt and pain, she desired to lash back with a repertoire of her own hurtful words. Closing her eyes and biting her lip, she hoped to resist the temptation. Remaining calm would not be an easy project for she hated being hurt.

"Give her My quiet Spirit," Jesus cried in intercession. "Help her understand that a quiet spirit and a gentle word turns away wrath. Spirit, give her the help she needs."

One of my own personal struggles manifests itself in this area. Retaliation and justification pop out of my mouth faster than popcorn in a microwave. I have grieved, groaned and grappled with the frustrations of spouting off rather than maintaining a tight lip.

Peace in this area did not begin to settle in my being until a study of Scripture revealed His power and His supply. The choice to change rested in me. The power to change rested in Him. The process of change rests in these three steps:

1. Come to a quiet place.

   Psalm 37:7a ____

   ____

   Psalm 46:10-11 ____

   ____

   Mark 6:31 ____

   ____

2. Center your daily life in and on Christ.
   Mark 4:39 ______________________________________
   ____
   John 14:27 ______________________________________
   ____
   John 16:33 ______________________________________
   ____
   Ephesians 2:14a ______________________________________
   ____
   Colossians 3:1-3 ______________________________________
   ____
   Hebrews 12:1-3 ______________________________________
   ____

3. Rely on the Bridegroom to make the changes.
   Psalm 143:7-10 ______________________________________
   ____
   Isaiah 26:3-4 ______________________________________
   ____
   Lamentations 3:26 ______________________________________
   ____
   Romans 8:6b ______________________________________
   ____
   Philippians 4:7 ______________________________________
   ____
   Colossians 3:15 ______________________________________
   ____

While it is difficult to understand how this change can take place, we must believe it can and will be done. We rejoice that our precious Bridegroom and the Holy Spirit can and will work His mighty miracles in us. In tenderness, He touches us and says, "Be still and know that I am God. Put your trust in Me."

PRAYER: Dear Jesus, I cannot adequately express the gratitude I feel for the miracles You create in this stubborn, aggressive spirit of mine. As I praise You for Your faithfulness and patience, create in me a spirit that reflects Your quietness and patience. Give me the courage to listen to Your Spirit when challenged and to accept Your power to resist. In Your name, I pray. Amen.

Chapter 10 — FREEDOM FROM FEAR

The flight began routinely. But several hours after our departure and only about 100 miles from home, we began to feel the effects of what was to become a turbulent and dangerous storm. Feelings of helplessness and fear swept over me. The silence of others on the plane seemed excruciating. The plane bounced around like a toy in the hands of a small child. Lightening struck the plane, lighting it up like a Christmas tree, sending shudders down my spine with the fear of a very unpleasant death.

Grasping the arms of the seat with all the strength I could muster, I began singing hymns and quoting every Bible verse I could remember. I didn't know what would happen, but I knew the One who did. In the midst of fear, I knew He was my only place to turn.

Fear – the undesired emotion! It creates terror in our very being and, in some circumstances and in some individuals, it can even be crippling. Those who encountered severe trauma or are continually stunned by phobias understand better than anyone the devastating effects of fear.

Yet God continues to say, "Fear not." But in order to do that, we need first to understand and possess another type of fear – and awesome respect, adoration and reverence for the great "I AM."

The Scripture references below contain loving promises granted to you by the Bridegroom when that awesome fear exists. List those promises.

Psalm 25:14
Psalm 31:19-20a
Psalm 34:8-9
Psalm 103:11-13,17a
Psalm 111:5,10
Psalm 145:18-19

Not only is the fear of God associated with a deep appreciation of who He is but also with the wisdom gained through that awesome fear. Solomon, the wisest man who ever lived, offered his advice in Proverbs 2:1-6. Take note of the "if – then" process needed to receive understanding and knowledge. Are you willing to surrender to that respectful fear in order to conquer your negative fears?

Read the following sections of Scripture to verify the various fears He promises to eliminate.

Judgment – 1 John 4:17-18

Storms, whether in nature or in life – Matthew 8:23-26, Matthew 14:22-33

Sharing the goodness of Christ with others – Acts 18:9-11

Moving on to new circumstances – Deuteronomy 31:6,8

Depression, Despair – Psalm 118:5-6a

Fear of others – Psalm 27:1, 13-14

Bad news – Psalm 112:5-8

Weakness – Isaiah 41:9b-10

Terrifying circumstances – Isaiah 43:1b-3a

Catastrophes of nature – Psalm 46:1-3

God's rejection – Romans 8:31-39

In the midst of fear, Christ your Bridegroom promises peace and rest. Read His words of comfort in John 16:33 and John 14:27.

To conclude this lesson, read Psalm 91. List all the blessings bestowed upon you for waiting on His righteous right hand.

PRAYER: Precious Jesus, thank You for being an ever-abiding presence within me. As I struggle with fears, both real and imaginary, grant me Your power and strength to trust, rest, and submit to You. Thank You for Your patience and unconditional love that constantly awaits my desire for freedom in You. Grant me Your peace in the midst of all fear and Your courage to overcome. Amen.

Chapter 11 — A TRUSTING HEART

How easily young children trust their parents! Without question, they believe to be true every promise made, every comforting word stated, and every fair decision offered. A glance, a touch or a hug is all they need to calm their troubled spirits and elevate joy in the midst of their emotional fears.

That same child-like trust is possible in the presence of Jesus Christ. Understanding that we are the Bride of a King, we rest secure in His glance of love through inner peace, His touch of comfort through His Word, and His hug of reassurance through prayer.

Words of comfort and assurance are evident often in Scripture. But the Psalms are exceptionally explicit in declaring the gentle blessings granted to those who trust Him. As you search for these blessings in the following passages, take time to meditate on how they apply to you in your own life.

Psalm 9:10
Psalm 22:5
Psalm 28:7-9
Psalm 31:14-16
Psalm 32:10b
Psalm 37:3-7a
Psalm 62:1,8
Psalm 125:1
Psalm 143:8,10

One of the greatest promises in Scripture wraps a believer in comforting words of the Bridegroom's assurance. Believing and accepting this promise as true opens wide the doors for trust. Read Jeremiah 29:11-13 and fill in the missing blanks:

"For I know the plans I have for you," declares the Lord, "plans to __________ you and not to __________ you, plans to give you __________ and a __________. Then you will __________ upon me and come and __________ to me, and I will __________ to you.

You will __________ me and __________ me when you seek me with all your __________."

His tender eye is forever focused on granting us His unconditional love. His promises to grant us a hope, a future – to listen when we pray – to reveal Himself to those who avidly seek Him – are constant, secure and stable. While situations in our lives may crumble, His rock-like strength will never falter. His timing, based on His eternal wisdom, will strike us like finely tuned chimes in a beautiful clock. And all it takes is our trust and our willingness to cry, "Help," when the trust is shaky. By doing so, we discover strength from Him to proclaim His praises in the midst of the trial.

Declare His goodness as you study the following verses about trust and remember that trust restores our inner being with peace – a peace beyond understanding.

Psalm 40:3-4a
Psalm 52:8-9
Psalm 56:3-4
Isaiah 12:2

Conclude this study by memorizing Isaiah 26:3-4. Use these verses to claim His promises on every occasion of stress and despair, of decision and direction. Trust in the Bridegroom, the Rock eternal.

PRAYER: Father, it is so hard to trust when the world offers so many avenues of self-security. Circling my life with earthly comforts and protection, I become assured in my own control – my own false hope. Through Your Spirit, reveal that true treasures are found not in self or in the things of this life, but in You. Help my unbelief as I make the choice to draw nearer to You daily. Reward me with the blessings of the Bridegroom as I continue in my walk of trust with You. In Jesus name, I pray. Amen.

Chapter 12 — UNRELENTING LOVE

My newborn daughter appeared tiny and fragile. Wrapped snugly in a blanket, she appeared like an emerging butterfly from its cocoon, yet her beauty far exceeded any other creature I had seen. Her tiny hands, held close to her face, displayed minute fingernails and slender, thin fingers. The curly, brown hair crowned her head and the pink, fair skin highlighted her precious face, so precious to behold.

What mother hasn't beheld the awesome beauty of her firstborn child and shed tears of amazement and gratitude for the prize held in her arms? Nothing compares to it. Nothing erases its memory. The wonder of instant love sends shudders of immense pleasure and joy through every fiber of a woman's body as she beholds this wondrous miracle.

I believe that in the heart of God, each child born – no matter the gender, the size, or the external appearances – invokes the same awe and amazement to Him as to the earthly parent – only His love and affection is far beyond any that man can comprehend. Each child gains a place of special place attention in His nursery of love. Each is offered the blessing of eternal life. Each is deeply loved.

To prove that love, the Bridegroom gave up His life in complete sacrifice for the sins yet to come. Unfailing love dominates the life-blood of Christ as He constantly and continually intercedes for them. Precious in His sight, He too sheds tears at their presence on earth. He too desires to cradle them in His arms. He too shudders with immense joy at this creation and yearns to have them draw into His presence.

To better understand that love, look up the following verses. Record the pleasures found by those who surrender to that love.

Psalm 6:4
Psalm 21:7
Psalm 32:10
Psalm 33:5,22
Psalm 36:5,7,10
Psalm 40:11
Psalm 63:3-4
Psalm 86:5,13,15
Psalm 90:14
Psalm 103:8,11

Difficult to fathom, the unrelenting love of the Bridegroom far exceeds our imaginations. He demonstrates that love to us not only in His one-time covenant sacrifice for us on the cross, but in His continuous, eternal supply of it.

As you study the following verses, record the ways He is revealing an example for us to follow, giving directions for loving others, and/or offering His unending source of supply.

1 John 2:5-6
1 John 3:16-18
1 John 4:7-16
1 John 5:2-5

Specifically mentioned in 1 John 5 is the phrase "and his commands are not burdensome." As His power generates love in and through us, a transformation takes place. The more love we give away, however sacrificial, the more love we have to give. There is no end to the supply. That love then creates an attitude of gratefulness for the privilege of being His child. That love, given away, creates satisfaction and joy; it is now a pleasure to serve Him in this manner. We become enabled to do the impossible, to react differently than our selfish natures once craved. Look for those changes as you study the following passages.

Matthew 5:44-45a
Matthew 22:37-39
John 13:34-35
John 15:9-19
1 Thessalonians 3:12
2 Thessalonians 3:5
1 Peter 1:22
1 Peter 4:8

This love is like a generator that stays closely connected to the power source, Jesus Christ. As you close this study, meditate on the unrelenting love that your Bridegroom revealed to you and to each child born on this earth. Revel in His goodness and rest secure in His love.

Lamentations 3:22
Zepheniah 3:17
2 Corinthians 5:14-15
1 Timothy 1:14
Romans 5:8
1 John 3:1

PRAYER: Bathed in Your love, dear Jesus, I come to You pleading for the faith to accept Your presence in my life. Open my heart and mind to the all-consuming, unrelenting love that You freely offer. Draw me into Your presence and flood my spirit with the love that surpasses knowledge. Grant me Your Spirit that may I forever fix my eyes on You and accept all that You desire to give me. In Your name, I pray. Amen.

Chapter 13 — HIS FULLNESS

Circumstances in our lives either propel us to trust in a loving God or repel us away from Him. A recent TV show portrayed a high-governing official, rejecting God because of the death of a dear friend and co-worker. He revealed anger and bitterness. Believing her death to be God's reaction to his own inadequacies and mistakes in his political life, he intentionally turned his back on God and desecrated, in a small way, the church in which he entered.

Unfortunately, the despairing questions about the heart-breaking events of our lives turn many away from God in the same way. Rather than rest in His wisdom, they reject Him and turn their backs on Him and His church. Believing the church and fellow believers to represent His indwelling, His fullness, they repel away from anything that represents God. In so doing, they cut themselves off from viewing the fullness available to them in the midst of the difficulties.

Read the following verses and acknowledge the "fullness" available in and through our Bridegroom.

Psalm 4:7-8
Psalm 48:10
Psalm 119:64
Acts 14:17

His fullness never exists without His all-powerful, all-consuming love. He craves and desires to display His goodness, even in the trials and tribulations of life. Available to us for the asking, His love is accompanied with a willingness to fill us to overflowing with His abiding presence.

Discover the connection between the abundant love of Jesus Christ and His fullness. Meditate on it as you read the following Scripture references.

Ephesians 3:16-19 (esp. verse 19)
Ephesians 4:13
Colossians 1:19,25
Colossians 2:9-10
John 1:16

The breaking points, the devastating realities, and the misunderstood events can be surrendered into His loving hands. In exchange for a willingness to yield to His wisdom, we recognize His unfailing love and power.

Discover the privileges of being filled by Him through His Holy Spirit.

Psalm 130:7
John 17:13
Acts 6:5,8
Acts 11:24
Romans 15:29
Ephesians 5:18b
Colossians 2:2

Resist the temptation to repel away from His fullness. Rather, pray that His Spirit will propel you to trust – even when it doesn't make sense. Express your desire of faith in these words of Peter: *Though we have not seen him, we love him; and even though we do not see him now, we believe in him and are filled with an inexpressible and glorious joy, for we are receiving the goal of our faith, the salvation of our souls* (1 Peter 1:8-9).

PRAYER: Holy Father, it is with grateful heart that I surrender my needy, crying heart to You. Desiring to be filled with the Spirit and all the fullness of my Bridegroom, I rest in Your decision-making to teach me how to apply my heart unto wisdom – Your wisdom. May my love abound more and more in knowledge and depth of insight, so that (I) may be able to discern what is best and may be pure and blameless until the day of Christ, filled with the fruit of righteousness that Jesus Christ – to the glory and praise of God. Amen (Philippians 1:9-11, pronoun change made).

Chapter 14 — ETERNAL LIFE

Spas, health clubs, the YMCA, and health food stores do a booming business today. With the desire of a large portion of our population to be that of maintaining a healthy existence, these locations explode with people. Their hopes – to live longer and look better.

The fountain of youth, long sought after, now comes to reality more than ever before. Plastic surgeons fix up, fill up, and flatten down desired parts of the body that begin to sag, droop and flop. Miracle drugs, potions and oils entice men and women to spend thousands of dollars, all hoping to restore their outward, youthful appearance. Skin peels, laser surgery and harsh scrubs add to the list of procedures attempted in hopes of erasing the wrinkles and smoothing the skin.

Also promised and, in many cases effective, is the influx of drugs to prolong life and eradicate the effects of aging on our bodies. And it's working! People are living longer and are more productive after the age of sixty-five than ever before.

Yet no matter how many processes, procedures, and pills we pop and in which we participate, we will still all die – it is the way of life. All the earthly steps we take to prolong life will still come to an end. Nothing provides an eternal remedy for aging and death.

But life – abundant life – can be eternal. Although not physically here and now, it is promised spiritually. In 2 Corinthians 4:16, the inward renewal is contrasted with the outward wasting away. Both are real – both continue to happen. But the victory rests in knowing that the inward renewal activates and energizes our spirit today and continues to eternity. Discover the wonders of inward, eternal renewal.

Psalm 16:11
Psalm 21:6
John 4:14
John 10:27-30
Romans 6:22-23
2 Corinthians 4:17-18

An amazing section of Scripture that is deserving of meditation and contemplation is Titus 3:4-7. Fill in the missing words and take time to focus on those words as you do so.

But when the __________ and __________ of God our Savior appeared, He __________ us, not because of righteous things we had done, but because of His __________. He __________ us through the washing of __________ and __________ by the Holy Spirit, whom He __________ out on us __________ through Jesus Christ our Savior, so that having been __________ by His __________, we might become heirs having the __________ of __________ __________.

Jesus sent the Holy Spirit to us with a mission – to wash us through rebirth and renewal, to pour out on us **generously** the eternal presence of Jesus Christ. In Him, then, is eternity.

What does Jesus say about Himself in the following references?

John 11:25
John 14:6

Jesus **IS** the life. He is the eternity we seek. When He dwells in us, we possess eternal life. What words in John 6:40, John 10:27-28, and John 17:3 support that?

As you grasp the Word, in which He dwells, determine to seek eternal life – the resurrected, eternal Bridegroom. *Fight the good fight of faith. Take hold of the eternal life to which you were called* (1 Timothy 6:12a).

Witness for yourself the presence of Life as you agree with John, His beloved disciple. As he saw the true Life revealed in Christ, he announced, *That which was from the beginning, which we have heard, which we have seen with our eyes, which we have looked at and our hands have touched – this we proclaim concerning the Word of life. The life appeared; we have seen it and testify to it, and we proclaim to you the eternal life, which was with the Father has appeared to us* (1 John 1:1-2).

PRAYER: Amazing, eternal Jesus, I praise You for the pleasures and joy that abound at Your right hand. Open my eyes to the eternity of blessings bestowed on those who love You. Then burden our hearts to pass it on – to share it abundantly – that Your eternal pleasures may flow on to others. Through Your Holy Spirit, enable us to fix our eyes on You – now and for eternity. In Your name, I pray. Amen.

Endnotes

[1] Edward Everett Hale, quoted by Vern McLellan, *Sensible Sayings and Wacky Wit* (Wheaton, Ill: Tyndale House Publishers, Inc., 1998)

[2] Doris Lessing, quoted by Vern McLellan, *Sensible Sayings and Wacky Wit* (Wheaton, Ill: Tyndale House Publishers, Inc., 1998)

[3] *The Handbook of Bible Application*, Neil Wilson, Ed. (Wheaton, Ill: Tyndale House Publisher, Inc., 1992), p. 469

[4] *1001 Humorous Illustrations*, Michael Hodgin (Grand Rapids, MI: Zondervan Publishing House, 1994), p. 77

[5] Ibid., p. 156

[6] Ibid., p. 442

[7] Ibid., p. 246-247

SDG

Notes

Notes

Notes